An Ethos of Transdisciplinarity

An Ethos of Transdisciplinarity

Conversations with Toyin Falola

Sanya Osha

ANTHEM PRESS

Anthem Press
An imprint of Wimbledon Publishing Company
www.anthempress.com

This edition first published in UK and USA 2025
by ANTHEM PRESS
75–76 Blackfriars Road, London SE1 8HA, UK
or PO Box 9779, London SW19 7ZG, UK
and
244 Madison Ave #116, New York, NY 10016, USA

© Sanya Osha 2025

The author asserts the moral right to be identified as the author of this work.

All rights reserved. Without limiting the rights under copyright reserved above,
no part of this publication may be reproduced, stored or introduced into
a retrieval system, or transmitted, in any form or by any means
(electronic, mechanical, photocopying, recording or otherwise),
without the prior written permission of both the copyright
owner and the above publisher of this book.

British Library Cataloguing-in-Publication Data
A catalogue record for this book is available from the British Library.

Library of Congress Cataloging-in-Publication Data: 2024949043
A catalog record for this book has been requested.

ISBN-13: 978-1-83999-320-6 (Hbk)
ISBN-10: 1-83999-320-0 (Hbk)

Credit: Photo Credit Michael Efionayi

This title is also available as an e-book.

CONTENTS

Part 1: A Long Introduction Divided into Several Segments   1

    Introduction   3

    The Yoruba: Falola's Tactile Ethnic Home   9

    Toyin Falola, Public Engagement and an Exercise in Pan-Africanism   15

    Scholarship of Transdisciplinarity and Interculturality   19

    The Significance of Orisa   29

    Unfinished Business   37

    Bibliography   39

Part 2: An interview section   53

    A Conversation with Toyin Falola   55

Index   183

Part 1

A LONG INTRODUCTION DIVIDED INTO SEVERAL SEGMENTS

INTRODUCTION

Toyin Falola, an extraordinarily prolific historian, is undoubtedly an astonishing academic phenomenon of our times. Over the past four decades, the Nigerian-born scholar has contributed significantly to virtually all the disciplines in the humanities and social sciences spanning history (ancient, modern and contemporary), political science, art theory, poetry, literary criticism, anthropology, sociology, philosophy, gender studies, ethnic studies, globalization studies, ethnology, and the related disciplines of African and black diasporan studies. Such prodigiousness, versatility, and excellence in contemporary scholarship are rare, and therefore truly remarkable. But beyond the mere celebration of extraordinary academic achievement, there needs to be accompanying events to signpost and etch them in the annals of history.

Falola, in his work and life, affirms several African adages pertaining to the primacy of the collective ethos. The ancient African virtues and values of conviviality, communalism and reciprocity are central to his intellectual practice and lived experiences. An author, editor and co-editor of almost 200 academic volumes, his various intellectual projects have involved drawing together different African, Africa-descended and Africanist scholars of diverse ideological and theoretical persuasions in a bewildering assortment of collaborative ventures. Africa thus is not conceptualized as the homeland alone but viewed as part of an existential, historical, political and geostrategic continuum involving other black cultures in Europe, the United States, the Caribbean and South America.

This attests to a manifestation of Pan-Africanism in theory and practice. Falola is a Pan-Africanist of the activist stripe, and his global impact in this regard can be broadly perceived. In his numerous research projects in various parts of the Africana world, he developed life-long contacts and relationships with fellow travelers on the Pan-Africanist path. In thought and practice, he has diligently promoted the necessity and verities of Pan-African beliefs and philosophy. Africans everywhere are united through the disastrous histories of slavery, colonization, decolonization, and neocolonial oppression and their enduring legacies. Thus, if we are united in our forms of oppression, we should also stand together in overcoming them and building solid foundations for future generations. It is this kind of practical philosophy that is evident in Falola's intellectual practice and numerous extracurricular activities.

Apart from his sterling academic accomplishments, Falola is also keen on grassroots activities having been honored with several traditional chieftaincy titles on account of his involvement with various rural communities in his native Nigeria. He is interested in ancient and precolonial forms of knowledge, cultures, and practices, and a major part of his community engagements is geared toward the retrieval and revival of those repressed and frequently derided forms. Recently, he initiated the enormously successful Toyin Falola Interviews to explore and bridge the customary divide between town and ivory tower. This is a holistic approach to developing society along with its major institutions, practices, and strategic objectives and is also a key part of Falola's activities as an engaged and concerned citizen.

Falola's understanding of Pan-Africanism leads to a related philosophical and practical concept—humanism. Falola is also a humanist in the most profound sense of the term. An African notion of the concept is deeply but not exclusively related to the Southern African notion of ubuntu. This refers to the (re)affirmation of the self equally in communion with others. In other words, the individual attains full realization in conjunction with, and in consolidation of, the community. Falola consistently affirms the primacy of the collective and the communal ethos. It is in this light, that this essay seeks to critique and celebrate Falola's overriding humanism and communitarian spirit. Indeed this communitarian spirit operates at the broadest of levels bringing together friend and foe, rivals and collaborators, different races, countries, continents, and peoples in (re)defining the fundamental values and principles of human unity even in the face of stupendous heterogeneity and diversity.

Such ideological and conceptual beliefs constitute a vital aspect of Falola's ongoing intellectual project which this discussion seeks to explicate and complicate even further. I, therefore, seek to engage with various parts of Falola's vast corpus that highlight and invite critiques that address the conceptual issues bearing on his thought and practice. Since such intellectual inclusivity is also an integral aspect of Falola's work, I also seek to explore a multiplicity of conceptual, theoretical, and disciplinary approaches in this discussion. As Falola's work is interdisciplinary, multidisciplinary, and transdisciplinary in scope and intent, this essay hopefully intends to reflect and encompass this ethos of academic diversity and adventuresome inquiry.

Falola is a historian but I trained as a philosopher. I am not quite in a position to assess the validity of his historical methods. When I embarked on this project ten years ago, I had no idea of the actual scope of the project. As a philosopher, I am interested in recurrent theories, ideas and concepts in a scholar's work. Those are entirely what are useful to me as a philosopher. A scholar might be saying a lot of things on the surface across several books and publications but they might not be useful from a philosophical point of view. In short, for me as a philosopher, I am interested in the theoretical and conceptual merits of a scholar's work. These are largely the materials that are relevant to my own work. Unfortunately, Falola isn't that kind of scholar. True, he is an extraordinarily diverse and prolific scholar but how much of his work is of use philosophically? This is a question I found myself constantly posing. But I am not going to make this kind of argument—that much of his work might be conceptually problematic—because it would obviously downplay his other strengths as a scholar. And so I came up with the idea that "transdisciplinarity" is a common motif pertaining to most of his writings. But I can only push this argument to a point until it also crumbles. If a really fastidious philosopher were to ask, what concepts or theories was he consistently advancing in his transdisciplinary writings, it would be hard to make a sustained argument. Indeed, there are many but they are not developed in a systematic or philosophically useful way.

Philosophers are trained to pose questions in quite specific ways. It is necessary to 'guard the question' in order to attend to the demands of "being." But in order to attend to this project, I had to set aside this fundamental *prolematique* and venture into a space of transdisciplinarity. I had to abandon momentarily a search for theory to be able to discover a different kind of fuel for discursive momentum.

The same kinds of questions could be raised about his project as a public intellectual. His work spans multiple media with different collaborators. But I am not interested in his collaborators because we are interested in Falola's ideas solely which are almost impossible to pin down. When I was working on this project, I published several articles and essays with the intention of building a coherent, overall argument on his work. It is another matter entirely whether I have been successful in this venture. Some of the articles that were meant to be part of the foundations of this book but ended up being discarded due to the pitfalls I have outlined earlier. The articles include but are not limited to:

"In remembrance of the slave" (parts I and II) https://journal.themissingslate.com/2016/02/15/in-remembrance-of-the-slave-part-ii-of-ii/
"Toyin Falola at seventy: A pan-Africanist luminary for the digital age" https://johannesburgreviewofbooks.com/2023/02/17/toyin-falola-at-seventy-a-pan-africanist-luminary-for-the-digital-age/

"Toyin Falola: 3 recent books that explain the work of Nigeria's famous decolonial scholar" https://theconversation.com/toyin-falola-3-recent-books-that-explain-the-work-of-nigerias-famous-decolonial-scholar-200851

"Toyin Falola's enchanted Yoruba universe: An Essay by Sanya Osha" https://www.africanwriter.com/toyin-falola-enchanted-yoruba-universe/

Indeed other essays and copious notes have been written but remain unpublished, and these were also intended to be used for this book but can't be because they aren't theoretically or conceptually relevant to this project.

In order to overcome the difficulties I have been expressing, I requested for an interview with Falola and, fortunately, I was granted one. Hopefully, this interview demonstrates why Falola became the kind of scholar he is. As such, we hear from the proverbial horse's mouth the circumstances that led to him producing the kind of work he does.

In a nutshell, the book attempts three major things:

1. To weave an argument regarding the "transdisciplinary" features of Falola which happens to be the main object of the book.
2. To highlight some of Falola's strengths as a scholar which include his versatility (although not from a philosophical standpoint as this could also be problematic for a theory-driven venture).
3. By including an extensive interview with Falola, it is hoped that the interest of the general reader would be sustained and also demonstrate the cultural as well as intellectual circumstances that led to Falola's peculiar turn of mind.

It is tempting to suggest that Falola's versatility somewhat resembles Thoth's, the ancient Egyptian god of writing and wisdom and the creator of hieroglyphics. Thoth, who was said to have authored over one thousand volumes in diverse areas of intellection, was subsequently appropriated by both the Greeks and Romans and named as one of their own gods. In Greece, he was called Hermes, son of Zeus, the foremost messenger of the gods and the deity of oratory in his own right.

Perhaps even more than Chinua Achebe, Falola successfully delves into the heart of an indigenous African language, Yoruba, to revive its bounce, magic and innate rhythmic cadences. Achebe had complained in an interview granted to *The Paris Review* that the missionaries who translated the English bible into Igbo had murdered the fluidity of the language and had come up with a wooden version of it. In essence, written Igbo had been transformed into an unyielding bureaucratized relic of the originally spoken dialect.

Yoruba, in Falola's hands, meanders like tributaries away from its primal source to sing of its ancient glories and those of uncorrupted earth. When one senses the unfettered flow of a re-vitalized language even within the dominant strictures of a hegemonic idiom, one also feels the jubilation of the ancestors in connecting with the resumed current of life; for the spoken word is life and life feels most free when it emanates from the deepest, warmest bowels of language.

Ibadan, the city of Isola (one of Falola's numerous names), developed from being a war camp in the 1820s and was deservedly blessed with many renowned warriors. And in order to understand this historic city and its indigenes, it is necessary to know what Mesiogo means: "Mesiogo is a combination of two words pronounced as one, actually two words that should have been hyphenated in order to prevent confusion. *Mesi* is "to reply," but it is more than that; it is to be very quick to reply. *Ogo* means "a fool," someone stupid. In combination, Mesiogo communicates an ability to reply quickly to a fool, with actions and words that will communicate or disguise intentions" (Falola, 2013:73).

Proverbs, for the Mesiogo, represent the wings of conversation. Proverbs are not only replete with conceit, irony, delightful contradictions and conceptual resolutions, they are also repositories of folk wisdom, historical truths and powerful cultural markers. As such, they define and constantly refine the limits of collective identity. Falola employs them liberally: "White teeth do not mean the mouth would not smell " (Falola, 2013:165), "her tongue was a horse and she knew how to ride it" (Falola, 2013:168), sounds proverbial, " a man dashed to the floor by affliction should expect other insults to follow" (Falola, 2013:181), "he who marries beauty can marry trouble" (Falola, 2013:186), "a village cock knows not to crow in the city" (Falola, 2013:190) and "a roaring lion kills no game" (Falola, 2013:371).

Yoruba folklore is incomparably rich and riddled with fables about *abiku, emere, ogun owo, awure* (some of which will be explained later) and so on. The appeal of Falola lies in deftly conjuring that enchanted world to life. When that precarious world manages to breathe, modernity comes across as a brutal, drunken destroyer and as an insensitive substitute for a largely concealed universe of speech and belonging carefully arrayed by meaning, metaphor, and symbolism. Modernity is, to be sure, homogenizing in its basic tendency, while Falola's world embroiders and celebrates alterity and all the other subdued attributes that ostensibly undercut modernity's unparalleled dominance.

Unquestionably, the myths and history woven in Ibadan's antecedents possess epic resonance. The first leaders of the burgeoning settlement summoned a *babalawo* (a priest of Ifa) to offer revelations as to its future.

The *babalawo* in turn demanded two hundred snails which were released in all directions. The numerous trails came to signify the rapid growth of the war camp into West Africa's largest city in the nineteenth century and the global dispersal of its sons and daughters from the twentieth century onward. Ibadan has also become a magnet for people from far-flung regions of the globe.

When Isola Oloruntoyin Falola was born, the significance of the event was well-registered in his community. Prayers offered by all and sundry to Olorun, the supreme Godhead, to grant him "force, energy, vitality, power and drive." Olorun was also entreated to bestow the newborn child with other gifts besides. The prayers offered at Falola's birth were communal in nature with the effect of binding him fundamentally to his community's values and customs.

The wanderlust lodged in the hearts of the Mesiogo first manifested itself in the nine-year-old Falola who stole upon a train heading north toward Ilorin. At Ilorin, he disembarked and was quickly employed by a much older man who pretended to be a blind beggar. Falola survived for several days by serving as a pilot for the "blind" beggar until he was discovered by vigilant post office workers and promptly returned home.

THE YORUBA: FALOLA'S TACTILE ETHNIC HOME

Falola's most recent research traces the globalization of the Yoruba people in terms of history, culture, transformation, and change. Undoubtedly, this approach is a vast advancement on all previous similar projects, including that of Samuel Johnson's *History of the Yoruba*, which is a landmark work on the Yoruba in the late nineteenth century. The Yoruba are currently found in the southwest part of Nigeria, the Republic of Benin, Togo, Ghana, and Ivory Coast. Falola sets himself a dual problem: "What the Yoruba receive from the outside world (as in the cases of Islam and Christianity)" and "What they contribute to the world beyond them" (as in the case of Orisa and the Aladura/Pentecostal churches of Britain and the United States; Abimbola, 1973, 1975, 1976a, 1976b, 1977, 1981, 1998; Abiodun, 1975; Abraham, 1962; Addie, 1990; Adebisi, 1986; Adedeji, 1966; Adegbile, 1999; Adelugba, 1981; Adeoye, 1979, 1985; Adewoye, 1987; Afolabi, 2001; Afolayan, 2000; Ahye, 1981; Aiyejina & Rawle, 1999; Ajayi, 1974, 2000; Ajuwon, 1981; Akanmu, 1999; Akinjogbin, 1972; Akinjogbin, 2002, Akinjogbin, 1976; Akinyemi, 2004; Alade, 1992, 1995; Andrew, 1987; Atanda, 1980, 1973; Awe, 1973; Aweda 2002; Awolalu, 2001, 1979; Ayodeji, 1999; Babalola, 1966; Babayemi, 1973; Babayemi, 1979, 1976; Badejo, 1982, 2004; Balderson et al., 2002; Bamidele, 2003; Barber, 1989, 1981, 1979, 1984; Barnes, 1989; Bascom, 1973, 1969, 1972, 1980; Bastide, 1945, 1978, 1986; Baudin, 1884; Beier, 1994, 1959, 1980, 1960; Benkomo, 2000; Bettelheim, 2001; Bewaji, 1992; Biobaku, 1975; Birth, 1999; Bolaji, 1962; Bomfim, 1940; Borghero, 1865, 1997; Bourguignon, 2000; Bowen, 1858; Braga, 1992, 1995; Brain, 1980; Brereton, 1979; Browker, 1997; Brown, 2003; Burket, 1985).

In seeking to understand the origins, culture, and history of the Yoruba, Falola adopts the Akan concept of *Sankofa*, which means understanding the present via the lens of history. In exploring the rich historical experience of the Yoruba people, Falola's work surveys events spanning at least ten centuries. Beginning from ancient times, the Yoruba had interactions with their neighbors such as the Borgu, Benin, Nupe, Dahomey, the Hausa states and the Songhai Empire. Here, we glean evident traces of the multiculturalism and cosmopolitanism that would come to characterize the lives of many diasporic Yoruba. However, during the nineteenth century, the Yoruba people and towns were profoundly uprooted by the upheavals caused by the transatlantic slave trade and the much earlier trans-Saharan slave trade (Benkomo, 2000; Bettelheim, 2001; Bewaji, 1992; Biobaku, 1975; Birth, 1999; Bolaji, 1962; Bomfim, 1940; Borghero, 1865, 1997; Bourguignon, 2000; Bowen, 1858; Braga, 1992, 1995; Brain, 1980; Brereton, 1979; Browker, 1997; Brown, 2003; Burket, 1985; Cabrera, 1954; Campbell, 1989, 1995; Canizares, 2000; Capone, 1999; Carneiro, 1984; Carroll, 1967; Castor, 1999; Catherine 1997; Catholic Community Forum, 2005; Clapperton, 2005; Clake, 2004; Comaroff and John, 2004; Conner and David, 2004; Courlander, 1973, 1975; Daramola and Jeje 1970, 1967; Diamini, 1985, 1986; Drewal 1980; Drewel and Pemberton III, with Abiodun, 1989; Drewal, 1992; Dwyer, 1982; Egonwa, 1995; Ehret, 2002; Ellis, 1970; Eltis, 2004; Euba, 1990; Fadipe, 1991; Fakeye and Fakeye 1996; Fakinlede, 2003; Falola, 1999).

According to Falola, the Old Oyo Kingdom was an early entry point for influences such as Islam from the Maghreb, but the religion itself did not make significant headway until the eighteenth century. The Yoruba developed complex cultural and cosmological systems and practices such as the Ifa divination system, *egungun* (masquerade), the employment of cavalries, the craft of iron-making and sculpture through their varied interactions with the NOK, Nupe, Borgu, and Ado (Benin). In addition, the Yoruba developed a philosophical system incorporating *ori* (a form of spiritual determinism), *orisa*, and *Ifa*, which collectively define a unique tradition of epistemology. In order to understand an entire *episteme* involving philosophy, ethics, cosmology, history, and sociology, we need to understand the conceptual linkages between *ori, orisa*, and *Ifa*. Falola suggests we bear in mind these linkages.

The Yoruba epistemological and cosmological frameworks served as a bulwark against unrestrained Arabian and European cultural penetration. This is not to assert that the tripodal epistemologies of *Ifa, orisa*, and *ori* did not experience change, transformation, and epistemic destabilization with the advent of the highly disruptive transatlantic slave trade. The creation of the transnational Yoruba was facilitated by profound violence (the transatlantic slave trade) and other benign factors and circumstances, such as new-age cinematography and contemporary global digitalization. As such, Yoruba epistemological and cosmological elements are found in the

Afro-cultures of Cuba, Brazil, Trinidad and Tobago, the United States of America, Haiti, and other parts of America. Even Christianity, under the Yoruba influence, transformed into the Aladura movement, which is deeply marked by conceptual mutation and hybridity (Idowu, 1962, 2005, 2006, 2009; Ifaoogun, 2001; Isola, 2000, 1984, 1991, 1977, 1975, 1973; Itacy, 1989; Jackson, 2003; Johnson, 1966; Joseph and Mei-Mei, 2001; Joseph, 1987; Judith, 1971; Kerenyi, 2000; Kirsch, 2004; Klass, 1991; Klaus, 1996; Marks, 2001; Mason, 1992, 2002).

Essentially, Falola's most recent work explores the processes through which Yoruba identity has been shaped by globalized modernity. In terms of range and depth, a large portion of Falola's work also interrogates the history, people, traditions, religion, culture, and philosophy of the Yoruba. These issues would always be pertinent to all those interested in the history and culture of the Yoruba. Also, there has been a growing global awareness of decolonial studies with names such as Gayatri Spivak, Dipesh Chakrabarty, Walter Mignolo, Hamid Dabashi, Audre Lorde, Sara Ahmed, V. Y. Mudimbe, Paulin Hountondji, and Achille Mbembe receiving renewed critical attention as the new exemplars of decolonial thought. If we specifically examine the work of African scholars such as Hountondji and Mbembe, we would see that Falola's current thought reconfigures and advances the boundaries of decolonial thought for a number of obvious reasons.

Mbembe's supposedly decolonial *Critique of Black Reason* (2017) tackles his familiar concepts of the postcolony, "the fungibility and thingification" of the black subject, the current malleability and expansive of the concept of blackness, "human superfluity," the pluralities, mobilities, and modalities created by Afropolitan conditions and existence. But Mbembe's entire theoretical and conceptual framework seems to draw a great deal of his imagery from the same unreconstructed lens of colonialist anthropology. This prism portrays Africa as invariably "other(ed)," an unfathomable void, a site of delirium as explicated by Gilles Deleuze, a state of exception in which only the irredeemable can exist.

In Mbembe's world, the African, and by extension, the black subject, is supposedly devoid of identifiable agency and prey to forces (neuroscience, neuroeconomics, and animism) much larger than his/her radius of comprehension. These seemingly undecipherable forces necessarily include the modalities of post-Fordist capitalism and digital globalization. There seems to be no way out of this Kafkaesque nightmare, this elemental void of delirium, a state of exception larger than all states of exception. Within this entrenched conceptual vista the black subject is virtually reduced to being a mere "thing," in other words, a non-active subject of history.

It is necessary to present a counter-narrative to this ingrained dystopia which perennially presents Africa as a site of the irredeemable, a place of madness and irrationality. There is also the need to offer an alternative conceptual understanding of African global mobility, which is precisely the theoretical point of Falola's current research. The popular concept of Afropolitanism valorizes an elite circle of African cosmopolitans in exclusory power and privileges that determine one's right to existence (Falola and Matt 2004; Falola and Ann, 2005; Fatunsin, 1992; Ferreira, 2003; Folanrami, 2002a, 1995, 2000, 2002b).

Furthermore, the so-called Afropolitan way of life is unattainable for most Africans, and it glamorizes what the majority find abject and objectionable in terms of its accelerated consumerism and classism. Falola's work offers a different version of African mobility, migration, belonging, and subjectivity. It is a version that celebrates without being uncritical of the conditions of existence of diasporic Africans, which is characterized by considerable resilience, inventiveness, and agency. Moreso, it unveils a much larger canvas and history of these agential dynamics and unpacks the factors and modalities behind this astonishing resilience (Font 2005; Forbes 1851; Fosu, 1986; Foucault, 1991; Fraginals, 1976; Frobenius, 1968; Gibbons, 1999; Glazier, 1991, 1995, 1998, 1993; Gleason, 1971; Gotrick, 1984; Goveia, 1960; Greenfield and Andre, 2002; Grimes, 1994; Hall, 1971; Hancock, 1971; Hardt and Antonio, 2000; Hart 1957; Hartnoll, 1998; Hastrup, 1992; Henry, 2001, 2003; Hernandez-Reguant, 2022; Herbert, 1993; Herskovits, 1947; Herskovits, and Frances 1947; Hethersett, 1941; Higginbotham and River, 2002; Horn, 1981; Houk, 1995; Hugh, 1964; Hugh, 1983).

Undoubtely, much of Falola's thought bears intellectual antecedents that can be traced much further back to the Negritudist era of Leon Gontran-Damas, Leopold Sedar Senghor, and Aime Cesaire, whose *Discourse on Colonialism* attempts to pose the questions that Falola currently addresses: what is the breadth, extent, and depth of African subjectivity on a global scale? Falola argues that the depth of African humanity (and humanism) is much older, more resourceful, and deeper than most would assume. In providing such an affirmative response, Falola's larger project establishes a clear conceptual alternative within the burgeoning discourse of decolonial analysis in which the African is often shrouded in vagueness and conceptual silence.

Let us dwell briefly on some of Falola's more recent texts beginning with *African Spirituality, Politics, and Knowledge Systems: Sacred Words and Holy Realms* (2022). This book, he reveals was in part inspired by his interactions with a Canada-based Nigerian scholar, Samuel Oloruntoba. In Falola's words, "I would often call Sam, but he would be in his intense prayer session. He would answer the call, but he won't talk to let me know he was busy. He is a prayer warrior. He speaks in trance. I began to memorize his archaic words, which were impossible to decode. Then I would joke with him that he was reciting incantations, which I can do. Of course, this is blasphemy to him, but not to me. Incantations are hard to decode. The meanings of many words have been lost forever. None is fakery, except to atheists" (email communication, 2022).

In this book, Falola is interested in the spiritual power of the word, a concept not only familiar to Christianity but also Yoruba spirituality—in this sense, *ogede*, a ritual form of incantation with immense power—among other African spiritualities. He continues, "My favorite gospel of all time is *The Book of John*, and although there are debates about authorship, the earlier argument being that he must also have been the author of the Revelations. I see John as a professor in the way he layers the chapters, as if writing a dissertation around belief."

Instructively, while Falola is exploring African spiritual formations, he is also seeking out links to other cultural practices thereby affirming our common humanity and underlining certain continuities across multiple cultures. This is why he was able to perceive links between Christian worship and a manifestation of Orisa spirituality.

In 2022, Falola continues his extensive explorations of decolonial analysis in *Decolonizing African Knowledge*. This particular book is quite important not only for the South African context but also for regions going through various throes of decolonization.

We all know the often devastating impact European colonialism has had on the African continent as a whole. Slavery and the ensuing stages of neocolonialism have had a similar impact on all African communities.

Indeed what these harmful encounters have had on the African self was to effect a schism within it, as it were, a disconnect which has resulted in myriad forms of schizophrenia. In this project, Falola is attempting to heal the broken African self by bypassing archival sources proffered by colonial power. Instead, he commences a form of intellectual therapy by engaging with "alternative archives created by memory, spoken words, images and photographs." A key component in this regard is the use of autoethnography for recovering traces of African memory lost in the colonial haze.

The third major book by Falola in recent times is *African Memoirs and Cultural Representations* (2023). In this work, Falola focuses on the memoirs of West African writers who worked largely in the traditional vein, that is, largely outside the colonialist paradigm. In this manner, African perspectives, beliefs and norms are recuperated as a way of furthering a decolonial project. In addition, it highlights the nature and purity of the African voice beyond the colonial framework.

What these works do is to delineate Falola's positions regarding a global decolonial project, one that of course, also concerns South Africa after the #RhodesMustFall movement, which called for, among other things, a wide-ranging decolonial dispensation.

Instructively, these volumes are all single-authored. Falola has also co-edited recently, the Palgrave handbook on Islam in Africa and also a Palgrave Macmillan multi-volume project on women in Africa and African forms of feminism. Such is the scope, reach and impact of this exemplary African scholar who is simply peerless in this regard.

TOYIN FALOLA, PUBLIC ENGAGEMENT AND AN EXERCISE IN PAN-AFRICANISM

Thabo Mbeki, ex-president of South Africa (1999–2008), turned 80 years old on April 18, 2022. After a special event was organized at the Sandton Centre, Johannesburg, the Toyin Falola Interviews hosted another session of dialogues. The Toyin Falola Interviews is a remarkable forum that organizes public dialogues with highly distinguished Africans from all spheres of life most especially in politics, academia, social activism, culture and the arts. The Mbeki event was viewed by reportedly half of the South African population and over 30 million people worldwide including 13 heads of states across various countries. The session which also featured two young Nigerians, a poet and a singer, who honored Mbeki with their talents, lasted well over three hours.

Mbeki was interviewed by the renowned Malawian historian, Paul Zeleza and veteran South African TV anchorwoman, Naledi Moleo. Ultimately, Mbeki was warmly celebrated as an African giant, a true scion of Africa whose impact has been felt in several countries on the continent. Mbeki dwelled extensively on his various pet issues such as Pan-Africanism (repeatedly questioned by frequent xenophobic outbreaks in South Africa), the rebirth of the African National Congress, xenophobia, African renaissance, conflict resolution (solutions, Mbeki argued, come from ownership of conflict resolution processes). He touched on crises in the Democratic Republic of Congo, Rwanda, Cameroon, South Sudan, and Ivory Coast. Finally, he addressed the July 2021 riots in Durban and Johannesburg, the importance of active youth organizations to aid development, the educational crisis in South Africa, the challenges of the African Union (AU) (the decline of the AU's political commission after being subsumed under peace and security), neocolonialism, the G8, HIV/Aids (a major botch on his regime) and the COVID-19 pandemic.

The structure of the landmark Mbeki-Africa exchange was divided between South African affairs and broader continental issues. Zeleza and the rest of the audience who were invited to ask questions claimed Mbeki for the whole of Africa. Moleo tended to bring it all back home to South Africa.

South African Affairs

The Mandela and Mbeki administrations faced numerous challenges pertaining to building a new South Africa in the ashes of apartheid. The leaders of the African National Congress (ANC) had to confront and contain the incessant threats posed by counter-revolutionary forces who deemed "blacks unfit to rule." Just before the exit of the apartheid regime, the government instituted a social grants system that benefited only whites, colored and Indians to the exclusion of the black majority. The ANC had to devise a plan to ensure that blacks were also included in the scheme without also bankrupting the state which was in no position to fund such a massive welfare plan.

The Mbeki administration also had to deal with the HIV/Aids epidemic, which generated a lot of hostility and disagreement about measures to address it. Mbeki argued that there were many factors that led to decreased immunity such as acute malnutrition, prolonged and untreated disease and genetic factors among others. His plan was then to develop a holistic medical response to the HIV/Aids crisis for which he was labeled an HIV/Aids denialist.

Mbeki has often indicated his displeasure with the deadly fractionalization and lack of discipline that have come to characterize occurrences within the ANC whereby numerous political opportunists have managed to infiltrate the movement solely for the purpose of personal financial enrichment.

On the question of "handling over the baton to a new generation of South African leaders" as understood by Moleo, Mbeki pointed out there was no such thing as the issue of succession was a gradual and developmental process. He revealed he was incrementally groomed for leadership from his teens when Nelson Mandela would invite him for lunch to discuss knotty issues of policy and strategy in a roundabout manner, so to speak. In Mandela's eyes, Mbeki represented the promise of youth and the ANC leadership of yore encouraged and nurtured brilliance among its younger cadres.

Mbeki's Pan-Africanism is often problematic because of the repeated outbreaks of xenophobic violence which he incredulously denies exist in South Africa.

Pan-Africanism on Trial

Since leaving office as president of South Africa, Mbeki has not rested on his oars; traversing the continent on serial peacekeeping missions on behalf of the African Union (AU), planning dialogues with a wide variety of former and still serving African leaders (such as Paul Biya of Cameroon and Paul Kagame of Rwanda, two life-presidents) on continental issues of burning concern and indefatigably engaging with problems that threaten to implode upon the face of the continent.

Mbeki, ever the intellectual, confessed to having cited Zeleza several times in his deliberations and reflections. Mbeki, not surprisingly, has often been cast in the mold of African philosopher-kings such as Leopold Sedar Senghor, Kwame Nkrumah, and Julius Nyerere. At such an advanced age, there is still rigor, discipline, and precision with which he analyses intractable problems within the African continent and on a global level. And even at this late stage, his well-considered analyses are still highly sought after in Africa.

Indeed Mbeki serves as perhaps the most dynamic elder statesman on the continent, referring aggrieved Cameroonians to the Africa Commission comprising former presidents and other prominent African leaders to mediate the ongoing Cameroonian crisis that has pitted the Francophones against the Anglophones.

He dwelled on what has been called Africa's first world war in the Great Lakes Region where significant parts of the Democratic Republic of Congo (DRC) are engulfed by violence propelled by Rwandan and other forces. Mbeki seeks to consult with President Kagame on the matter.

Mbeki made decisive efforts at curbing the mayhem caused by the Ivorian crisis in which two presidential aspirants—Alassane Quattara and Laurent Gbagbo—were locked in a violent confrontation, which in turn led to a seemingly implacable constitutional deadlock. Mbeki has also been engaged in the conflict in South Sudan and strategies to end the civil war. He harped on the importance of consulting with all the relevant stakeholders and entrusting them with conflict resolution processes.

Asked about the mooted UK relocation of African refugees to Rwanda, Mbeki agrees the situation requires his urgent intervention. Again, he promised to consult with Kagame.

Africans from Cameroon, the DRC and Nigeria asked a lot of specific and general questions (more than 400 questions are to be forwarded to the Thabo Mbeki Foundation) pertaining to peace and security within the continent with Mbeki literally taking copious notes and pledging to do something about them. At the end of the exchange, it was clear that Mbeki had successfully transitioned from being an old mainstay of the African

National Congress (ANC) to a highly venerated and in-demand African elder trouble-shooter. And just as Nkrumah is, he is more respected on the continent than in his native South Africa. It was also obvious that he has evolved from a river which is South Africa to an ocean that is Africa. In spite of the apparent challenges of realizing the Pan-African ideal, Mbeki the octogenarian, remains a staunch Pan-Africanist.

In affirming and celebrating the role of a Pan-Africanist such as Mbeki, Falola is undoubtedly drawing attention to his own considerable stature as a Pan-Africanist and also underlining the primacy of Pan-Africanist ideology in the current global configuration.

SCHOLARSHIP OF TRANSDISCIPLINARITY AND INTERCULTURALITY

As mentioned earlier, Toyin Falola can arguably be called a public intellectual having achieved the status of Africa's most prolific and consistent historian. Of course, this would mean several things to different publics around the globe. Falola's Pan-Africanist outlook, activities and range have transformed him into a very unique type of scholar. He is indeed more than just a scholar and he has succeeded in redefining and expanding what it means to be a scholar-cum-activist-cum-public intellectual in an age of transnationalization. As noted earlier, his readiness to undertake works of remarkable quality in the genres of prose, poetry, cultural criticism, political commentary and of course, history, his initial and ostensible academic specialty, is particularly noteworthy. Although based in the United States, he visits Africa at least six times a year hosting conferences and organizing transnational research networks all over the continent.

By highlighting his terrifically versatile and prolific writings, it is necessary to focus on how the concepts of transnationality, interculturality, transdisciplinarity, locality and cosmopolitanism work within his output and how they can be employed in examining other outstanding scholars working on African(a)-related issues. It is also important to accentuate various ramifications of his multitudinous scholarly output.

Indeed, there is an aspect of his work that is often overlooked by scholars and even when studied is not as rigorously analyzed as other aspects of his corpus. This relates to his role, functions and achievements as a transdisciplinary scholar. To undertake an original analytical exploration of this crucial angle, means we have to go beyond the studies that have been produced on his intellectual life and work. Indeed it is possible to re-evaluate Falola's role as a transdisciplinary intellectual employing methodological grids that are quite novel. If for example, Falola has been concerning himself with important intellectual questions such as the transatlantic slave trade, colonialism,

African feminisms, postcolonial governance and contemporary African migrations to the North Atlantic hemisphere, then we have to go beyond the field of historical studies to engage with his work.

Apart from the questions outlined above, the other major research questions at this juncture are how has Falola addressed issues such as African precolonial heritage and marginalized or suppressed swathes of African history and existence? Indeed such matters are not to be left within the purview of historians alone. If these concepts belong properly to the domain of transdisciplinary studies, what is being done by specialists in the field to re-examine his contributions? Or rather what is the nature of the critical responses to his work on African diasporan issues? What are the long-term and short-term effects of Falola's transformation into a global public intellectual? What does this role entail? These are some of the research questions this book intends to tackle.

Indeed Toyin Falola's astounding intellectual production must be one of the mysteries in the intellectual world. It has transcended the confined world of historical research into broader horizons that include the role of the public intellectual. Any serious discussion of Falola's work needs to involve elaborate interrogations of the origins, continuities and discontinuities of his transformation as a public intellectual. This means we have to recast the debates regarding who is a public intellectual from a multiplicity of discursive situations and historical and cultural contexts. We have to employ methodological parallels from North Atlantic intellectual traditions. How did the role of the public intellectual emerge in the first place in world intellectual history? Addressing this question would enrich this research endeavor immensely.

In interrogating comparative discursive formations perhaps we also need to re-evaluate the roles, functions and achievements of continental intellectuals like Bertrand Russell, Jean-Paul Sartre, Andre Malraux, Albert Camus, Michel Foucault, Edward Said, Wole Soyinka and Pierre Bourdieu. Again this discursive element is a project other scholars and researchers need to undertake.

It also means a lot of importance is attached to the claim that Falola is a public intellectual of global importance. We would recall that as an intellectual Sartre wrote on and theorized issues relating to colonialism, racism and anti-Semitism. This made him a truly world-class intellectual. This book seeks to employ similar yardsticks in assessing Falola.

In the final analysis, it is necessary to assess the value and impacts of Falola's multidisciplinary and transdisciplinary engagements over the course of at least three decades. Such a comprehensive overview of his involvements has not been undertaken hence the value and justification of this book.

It is certainly necessary to reconsider Falola in light of his activities and accomplishments as a transnational as well as transdisciplinary public intellectual. Here, I attempt to offer a systematic interrogation of this issue. Ultimately, new discursive spaces will be broached and this would be good for even Falola himself in terms of his intellectual production and discursive realignments.

Toyin Falola's biographical and intellectual itinerary has been most interesting for one central reason: it subverts the myth concerning the African continent as an irredeemable ghetto. It also deftly bypasses common assumptions regarding Africa and the Africans as being inextricably tied to death, disease, decay and even delirium. This intervention seeks to better understand how Falola addresses the deterritorialization as well as the re-affirmation of the politics of identity. In other words, I am interested in the transnationalization of cultural subjectivity. This effort also addresses the connections—contained in Falola's project—between the imperatives of diasporan existence and continental Africa in a way that brings to the fore, a new sociocultural symbiosis, a new configuration of cultural synergies (Matory, 2005, 1994; Maulana, 1999; Mc Alister, 2002; Mc Daniel, 1998; McGee, 1983; Mc Leod, 1999; Memmi, 2006; Mendoza, 2015; Mintz, 1989; Mischel 1958; Morton, 1964; Murphy, and Mei-Mei,2001; Nasiru, 1989; Ndlovu-Gatsheni, 2000; Niane, 1965; Newson, 1976; Obafemi, 1996; Ogunbiyi, 1981; Ogunbowale, 1962; Ogundeji, 1998, 1988; Ogungbile, 2001; Ogunmola 1985; Ojo, 1969; Okediji, 1989, 1986; Olajubu, 1970, 1978; Olaoba,2005; Olatona, 2003; Olatunji, 1984; Olomo, 2003; Olukoju, 1997; Olunlade, 1961; Olupona, 2004, 1991; Omoniyi, 1987; Oriki, 1996;1995, 1954; Oyewumi, 1997; Palmie, 1993; Pares, 2006, 2004, 2005).

Instead of viewing Africa as a site devoid of hope, from Falola's account, we see an Africa that is effortlessly transnational and transcultural. And in being so, the African subject in effect assumes the same effortless transnationality and interculturality. Falola's cosmopolitan sensibilities are not a denial of his African roots. Indeed Africa remains a central and abiding preoccupation. For him, Africa remains the beginning of his journey and the site to which he continually returns to find all kinds of meaning: cultural, aesthetic, political and epistemological. In the exploration of these diverse meanings, Falola also bypasses the persistent nativism—in spite of his always evident Yoruba leanings and values—that confronts all of us who are compelled to subscribe to the politics of African identities and various ideologies of blackness. Falola affirms a politics of identity that recognizes the fluidity of all kinds of boundaries. It is also a stance that asserts, in subscribing to a particular cultural subjectivity we do not reject or denounce other cultural realities and boundaries. These are some of the directions to which Falola's ideological and cultural leanings attest.

The other perspective one gets from Falola's intellectual journey is the previously mentioned transdisciplinarity of his research projects. He begins his experience with writing as an academic historian and then moves on to transdisciplinary research. But his attitude has not been one that separates these various discursive domains. Rather, he is interested in exploring the connections between them. In other words, the distances that separate universes of discourse are to be traversed and not avoided. What connects one textual universe to another is usually more important than what separates them. Similarly what unities a continental African and a diasporic African is more important than the nature of geographical distance between them. Falola's current focus on issues and peoples of the diaspora ought to be read in this light. It is all part of the same transnationality, interculturality and cosmopolitanism which are all rooted in a particular site: Africa.

However, Falola's project can be made even more incisive by demonstrating how personal intellectual gains translate into wider African dividends. In other words, it is necessary to explore the broader social dimensions of the project as they relate to collective gain.

Falola's status as a public intellectual and as Africa's most prolific and consistent historian should not be taken at face value. Of course, this would mean several things to different publics around the globe. Falola's global outlook, activities and range have transformed him into a very unique type of scholar. He is indeed more than just a scholar as he has succeeded admirably well in redefining and expanding what it means to be a scholar-cum-public intellectual in an age of transnationalization.

By highlighting his terrifically versatile and prolific writings, it is necessary to focus on how the concepts of transnationality, interculturality, transdisciplinarity, locality and cosmopolitanism work within his output and how they can be employed in examining other outstanding scholars working on African(a)-related issues. It is also important to accentuate various ramifications of his multitudinous scholarly output.

In many ways, Falola addresses the sort of issues great twentieth-century intellectuals like Betrand Russell, Jean-Paul Sartre, Andre Malraux, Albert Camus, Michel Foucault, Edward Said, Wole Soyinka and Pierre Bourdieu confronted.

Falola's biographical and intellectual itinerary is rather interesting for one central reason: it subverts the notion of viewing Africa as a site devoid of constructive movement and dynamism. In Falola's account, we see an Africa that is effortlessly transnational and transcultural. And in being so, the African person in effect assumes the same effortless transnationality and interculturality. Falola's cosmopolitan sensibilities are not a denial of his African roots. Indeed Africa remains a central and an abiding preoccupation.

(Peel, 2000; Pemberton, 2000; Picton 2002; Pierson, 1971; Prince, 1964; Knight, 1970; Koch, 1974; Kwame, 1992, 1997; Lacerda, 1996; Ladipo, 1972; Ladipo, 1992; Landes, 1947; Lanternari, 1963; Larsen, 1983; Law, 1997, 1977; Lépine, 1982; Leuzinger, 1976; Lewis, 1971; Lima, 2005, 1977, 2000, 1966; Lloyd, 1971; Lody, 1998; Lovejoy, 2004; Lucas, 1948; Lum, 2000; Marcelin, 1996; Oyewumi, 1997; Palmie, 1993; Pares, 2006, 2004, 2005; Peel, 2000; Pemberton, 2000; Picton 2002; Pierson, 1971).

On a major level, his work covers so many disciplines, conceptual and theoretical terrains, diverse methodological approaches and geographical expanses beginning from Africa and its multiple diasporas to the world at large. This broader project encompassing numerous academic specialties, ideologies and multiple epochs underscores the prevalence of an ethos of communalism based on the African *weltanschauung*. As such, it immediately situates the communal teleology and consciousness above the individual subject. However, the author is only an individual and they have to affirm their individuality in order to make an undeniable claim to the ownership, that is, of their work. If we were to abide by this prescribed definition of ownership or property rights, then it becomes problematic to classify and describe Falola's enormously diverse bodies of writing. They constantly slip from our grasp and indeed our sights by virtue of their bewildering prolixity, mercuriality, transcendent intent, and innate subversion.

Unlike many other thinkers and theorists, on the surface, it is difficult to ascribe a distinct theoretical identity to Falola. Is it that theory is beyond him or that his work lies beyond the purview of theory? How does one theorize that which constantly re-writes and re-invents itself in the ordinarily inexorable effort to confront, and engage with, the dynamism of random existence and its varied phenomena?

This seemingly implacable proclivity to engage with the multitudinous prolixity and the unpredictability of existence locates its own theoretical axis in the African epistemology of holism; the absence of a distinction between mind and body, sensory and non-sensory, life and death or life and the afterlife. The very fact of life becomes a metaphysical project in itself.

Falola's work reflects this extra dimension of reality. And by extension, there is an abolition of the distinction between town and ivory tower, literate and illiterate, sacred and profane, the extraordinary and the mundane etc. There is an evident epistemology of holism at play as opposed to a paradigm of probably false binaries and distinctions (Matory, 2005, 1994; Maulana, 1999; Mc Alister, 2002; McDaniel, 1998; McGee, 1983; Mc Leod, 1999; Mintz, 1989; Mischel 1958; Morton, 1964; Murphy, and Mei-Mei, 2001; Nasiru, 1989; Niane, 1965; Newson, 1976; Obafemi, 1996; Ogunbiyi, 1981; Ogunbowale, 1962; Ogundeji, 1998, 1988; Ogungbile, 2001; Ogunmola 1985).

Thoth, the ancient Kemetian intellectual and metaphysical phenomenon is perhaps a philosophical forebear to Falola based on their shared extraordinarily diffuse practices, orientations and accomplishments. Thoth is reputed to have written over one thousand books in different areas of intellection and scholarly pursuits. His studies delved into the sciences, humanities as well as esoteric domains of knowledge (Ojo, 1969; Okediji, 1989, 1986; Olajubu, 1970, 1978; Olaoba, 2005; Olatona, 2003; Olatunji, 1984; Olomo, 2003; Olukoju, 1997; Olunlade, 1961; Olupona, 2004, 1991; Omoniyi, 1987; Oriki, 1996; Ortiz, 1995, 1984, 1995, 1954; Oyewumi, 1997; Palmie, 1993; Pares, 2006, 2004, 2005; Peel, 2000; Pemberton, 2000; Picton 2002; Pierson, 1971;; Prince, 1964; Knight, 1970; Koch, 1974; Kwame 1992, 1997; Lacerda, 1996; Ladipo, 1972; Ladipo, 1992; Landes, 1947; Lanternari, 1963; Larsen, 1983; Law, 1997, 1977; Lépine, 1982; Leuzinger, 1976; Lewis, 1971; Lima, 2005, 1977, 2000, 1966; Lloyd, 1971; Lody, 1998; Lovejoy, 2004; Lucas, 1948; Lugones, 2016; Lum, 2000; Marcelin, 1996).

However, the increasing compartmentalization of academic practices and the alienation created by a variety of modern forms of existence make it difficult to understand the epistemology of holism that undergirds Falola's academic practice. He is arguably a scholar who maintains an uneasy stance with the age of alienation, hyper-digitalization, compartmentalization and fragmentation. But this incompatibility is not due to an ultra-traditionalism, nativism or so-called primitivism. Rather, it stems from a certain recurrent sense of expansiveness contained in his work.

As such, it is imperative to appreciate the nexus of discursive concerns that inform Falola's epistemological architecture, intellectual practice and social activism.

The famed southwest Nigerian city of Ibadan is Falola's birthplace. Orisa spirituality, the communal ethos and a range of vernacular cosmopolitanisms coupled with an irreducible provincialism, diasporic Yoruba social formations and the problematic nation-state of Nigeria are primarily the cultural and political parameters that framed Falola's existential and discursive outlook. Of course, we must also mention Falola's incontrovertible belief in a Pan-Africanist intellectual and political project in addition to myriad forms of pluralism.

Nonetheless, his project is not about centralizing his voice or accentuating his own project alone. Indeed it is about the consistent empowering of voices of dissent and radical critique even when they are apparently contrary to his own stances. This is what makes his larger project essentially emancipatory.

As mentioned earlier, Falola's scholarship has produced almost 200 volumes encompassing disciplines such as philosophy, anthropology, sociology, political science, international relations, gender and sexuality studies, LGBTIQI+ activism, health care, spirituality, ethnic studies as well as every other subject that falls within the purvey of the social and human sciences. Indeed, his scholastic practice has no boundaries. Instead, it is eclectically broad while eschewing a wide variety of constraints both personal and professional. Ideologically, his practice seeks a liberty that questions and subverts its own justification at the same time.

Perhaps it should be stressed, once again, that an often baffling characteristic of Falola's prolixity is the apparent loss or sometimes even absence of theoretical coherence or potency. In his work, there is an evident belief in the attraction of volume, verbosity and gratuitous detail. Obviously, the maxim less is more is always discountenanced in favor of a Rabelaisian/Joycean expansiveness. If African philosophers, such as Kwasi Wiredu (1980), exemplified Spartan concision or a sort of Miles Davies-like post-bebop minimalism, Falola's represents the opposite end of the conceptual spectrum just as John Coltrane's cascading sheets of notes would.

However, the borderless limits of Falola's scholarship have both their merits and demerits. The most obvious delight associated with such a prodigious workload is its bounty of harvests; a quixotic cornucopia, a skewed amalgam of suspense, promissory pleasure and imminent reward. On the other hand, its greatest drawback has to be its resistance to structure and categorization and ultimately, the pleasures of theory and abstraction. Sometimes, when one ruminates on Falola's scholarship, so many subjects and perspectives flood the mind yet nothing really remains. Instead, a void unfurls amid nameless mists. But this is if one chooses to evaluate him within the all-too-predictable strictures of conventional scholarship.

Falola might argue that the discipline of history requires a multiplicity of discursive perspectives and a plethora of descriptive detail but surely his freewheeling transdisciplinarity exceeds the boundaries of historical requirements and expectations. And yet it is necessary not only to provide a discursive counterweight in terms of subject-matter but also a counter-narrative framework. Thus, as a counterweight to prolixity, there ought to be an accompanying quest for concision. Nonetheless, in the superficial appearance of an absence of theory, perhaps certain (quasi)theoretical parameters can also be established.

Instead, we need to connect with much earlier traditions of knowledge-making that date back to the Yoruba Ifa corpus, or Lagbayi, the transcendent Yoruba sculptor and intellectual, the glorious epoch of an itinerant artist/intellectual in precolonial Yoruba society (*are*) during the height of his cultural visibility, powers, and social capital. During such esteemed epochs in Yoruba cultural history, the public intellectual was obviously mysterious, given to subliminal vagrancy, intellectual retention and rebellion and yet he was also endowed with cultural primacy and potency.

In many ways, Falola encapsulates the figure of the *are* in indisputably postmodern times. Ever mobile, exploring ever-expanding frontiers of knowledge and intellection, Falola's indefatigability seems unreal.

As such, this introduction does not attempt to grapple with the entire range of Falola's scholarship. Instead, it seeks to depict the cultural, political and ideological backgrounds that molded his intellectual practices and outlook. There are also recurrent themes, subjects and concepts that prevail in his corpus.

The sprawling Ibadan metropolis is a good starting point. The city is shaped by both neoconservative and cosmopolitan elements that sometimes overlap even when they mostly appear to be separated. There are also important binaries to be considered in relation to Falola's work. Some of them include; academic and popular (both in terms of writings and copious activities), interdisciplinary and transdisciplinary, sole authorship and collaborative research.

In relation to Ibadan as a foremost site of cultural and intellectual ferment, there is also Nigeria and Africa and its multiple diasporas as spaces of much larger engagement and commitments. Conceptually, it is possible to move from Ibadan as a primal locus of investigation to the broader geographical space of Nigeria and eventually Africa and beyond.

Indeed there are multiple concepts that frame and animate these geographical spaces. Falola, in his writings and activities, always pursues an inexhaustible ethos of inclusivity in the form of communalism, communitarianism or unequivocal conviviality. The communal African self is instrumentalized through its multifaceted relations with others. Consequently, Falola invites us to read and interpret him through the values, concepts and ideologies he shares with other scholars. As such, his work is in constant conversation with other authors and thinkers. They are in fact innumerable.

The diverse range and styles of Falola's writings span elements of ethnography, snippets of biographical analysis, swathes of historical narrative, passages of subversive journalism as well as disavowed cosmological horizons and locations. In adopting this discursive trajectory, popular discourse melds with academic treatise, high and low culture, public knowledge and personal recollections, Falola's insights and those of his numerous collaborators, all these facets are ingrained in his scholarship and add to its distinctive cadence, identity and orientation.

Furthermore, Falola's scholarship, social engagements and philosophy seek to capture an essence; a fleeting essence of humanity in its splendorous multiplicity: good and evil, morality and immorality, femininity and masculinity, God and deity, heterosexuality and LGBTQI+ community, belonging and alienation, Africa, Europe and the world. In order to reflect this range of discursive interests, a propulsive mindset of human inclusivity and diversity is required.

Also at play is the same ethos of inclusivity and the centrifugalized self that pursues its limits beyond the boundaries upon which it dissolves itself. Conceptually, it is necessary to comprehend the multiple dimensions of Falola's prolixity. In order to understand such a fundamental characteristic, it is also necessary to locate a thematic and theoretical structure within his boundless prodigiousness by identifying a commonality of subjects and motifs based on culture, rusticity, urbanity, inclusivity, esotericism, nationalism and the Pan-African ideal. Indeed some of these attributes and categories are of course not only contradictory but also necessary ingredients in establishing a recurrent discursive as well as ideological blueprint. Thus, in ascribing a form of structurality upon what appears to be discursive formlessness, it is then possible to define an epistemology, in other words, to delineate an essential epistemology of holism. Here, the role and place of the Cartesian ego are subsequently reversed, and the collective "We" takes precedence by establishing its irrefutable centrality and open-ended circumference. Subsequently, the individuated self (re)activates its presence by wending its way within the parameters defined by the broader collective being. In his life, work and public and personal engagements, Falola is an exemplar of this foundational and self-evident axiom.

And just as he burrows through multiple disciplines with great rapidity, frequency and width, so does he shuttle across numerous geographical landscapes and cultural settings in more or less the same manner.

THE SIGNIFICANCE OF ORISA

Sango, the popular Yoruba deity, is worshipped in many parts of the world where footprints of Yoruba culture are to be discerned. Such footprints litter wide swathes of West Africa and of course, the Americas which were a key destination during the transatlantic slave trade. And through the global dispersal of the Yoruba during the slave trade, their religion, often referred to as *orisa*, became a widely known system of worship and veneration. The number of Yoruba deities has been put at 401 but it is advised that this should be regarded as a metaphorical ascription rather than actual computational truth. Many deities are duplicated in various communities and this would account for their initial prolixity.

However, it is mostly agreed that the objects of spiritual veneration are not more than 200. *Orisa* are categorized into two broad classifications namely canonized forebears or deified elements of nature such as earth, wind and fire. They are further divided into metaphorically white deities (*orisa funfun*) such as Obatala, Osun, Yemoja, Olokun and Osoosi and hot deities (*orisa gbigbona*), most notably, Ogun, Sango, Osanyin/Obaluaye and Oya. White deities are often described as "gentle, soothing, calm, and reflective."[1] Hot or temperamental deities, on the other hand, are notably "harsh, demanding, aggressive, and quick tempered."[2]

It is instructive to note that *orisa* are not classified according to a vertical hierarchy or order of superiority and all of them are known to have both positive and negative attributes. It is also useful to mention that "the relative importance of any *orisa* in any given part of Yorubaland reflects the deity's relative local popularity, reputation, and influence."[3] Nonetheless, the extent of influence and veneration each deity enjoys worldwide differs. For instance, deities such as Ogun, Sango, Obatala, Osun, and Oya are indeed venerated globally (Ramos, 1987; Ramos, 1996; Reis, 2003; Reis and Ecuardo, 1989; Ribeiro, 2005, 1987; Rodriguez, 1977, 1995, 1997; Roland, 1988; Saburi, 1973; Samuel, 1852, 1921a, 1921b).

Sango, specifically, is deemed to be most potent and most feared both within the traditional Yoruba homelands of West Africa and in the diaspora.

His acolytes in Trinidad and Tobago refer to him as "Papa Sango" as a term of endearment. The cult of Sango is manned by a group of priests known as *mogbas* and has the *ona-mogba*, and he works with two key assistants known as *otuun-mogba* and *osii-mogba*. The priests of the cult routinely perform magical feats to inspire and attract new adherents to the cult, and they also serve as mediums through which to communicate with the deity.

There are two ways in which Sango is worshipped, notably, through periodic and annual festivals and this differs slightly in his traditional homesteads in West Africa and the diaspora. Sango rituals are usually brief and occur once a week. While in the diaspora, they are held on Thursday or Friday; in Yoruba land, it is held on the last day of the traditional four-day week on Jakuta day, that is, on the day Sango fights with stones. An important of the ritual worship of Sango is *orisa wiwe*, in which the deity is bathed symbolically employing a herbal treatment derived from *eesun* (*Pennisetum purperedum* Schum), *tete* (*Amaranthus hybridu* Linn), *odundun* (*Bryophylliam*), and water is collected from the *ojubo* (the altar). An essential part of the ritual worship of Sango is the invocations of his name through incantations and praise songs. A ram and cock are then slaughtered and their blood is poured on the paraphernalia of worship. Their blood is meant to elicit the potency of Sango. The flesh of the slaughtered animals is then cooked and devoured by devotees present at the shrine.

At the end of the ritual worship of Sango, his priests and devotees leave the shrine and move to the precincts of the town, offering prayers to the ancestors and benediction to the town and its people which eventually culminates in the public performance of magical feats by the priests of Sango to both entertain and inspire the spectators at the event.

Yoruba *orisa* spirituality is essentially polytheistic and while the practice cannot be said to be growing, it is also spreading in significant numbers. The academic reception of the spirituality has not been particularly encouraging among atheists and agnostics, while scholars of religion(s) tend to view devotees of traditional Yoruba spirituality as unsophisticated adherents, worthy of perhaps, only mild bemusement.

As noted previously, it is sometimes tempting to admit that Falola's versatility somewhat resembles Thoth's, the ancient Egyptian god of tongue and creator of hieroglyphics. (Sandoval, 2000; Sandra, 1989, 1980a, 1980b; Sansi, 2007; Santos, 1994; Santos and Santos, 1981; Santos, 2001; Santos and Manoel, 1989; Schiltz, 1982, 1980; da Silveira, 2000, 2004; Simpson, 1980; Smith, 1969; Sobande, 1978; Soyinka, 1976; Sublette, 2004; Tavares, 2000; Thieme, 1969; Thompson, 1984, 1970; Thornton, 1983; Taiwo, 2005; Timi, 1961; Tishken, 2000; Tobe, 2003;; Toyin, 2006; Trigger, 2003; Trotman, 1976; Tsing 2000; Van, 2005; Verger, 1999, 1981; Visona, 2000; Wafer, 1996;

Warner-Lewis, 1996; Welch, 2001; Wescott and Peter 1962; Whitford, 1967; William, 1969; William and Moses, 2008; Wiredu, 1980; Wood, 1968; Yai, 2001; Young, 1995; Zuesse, 1979).

One of the most telling and endearing traits of Falola in spite of his vast knowledge base is a capacity and willingness to learn. In our conversations, he has this almost eerie ability to do far more listening than talking. As such, conversations with him are not occasions for ego-boosting and pedantic antics. Instead, they are opportunities to foster camaraderie, discreet doses of repartee and mutual edification.

In his several book series for publishing houses such as Rochester University Press, Palgrave Macmillan, Cambridge University Press, Rowman and Littlefield, Bloomsbury Academic, Routledge and many other important presses, Falola constantly strives to connect African peoples with their sis/brethren in multiple diasporas. Such interactions are often marked by intense conviviality, reciprocity, dialogue and critical analyses. Through these various book series, Falola initiates and executes numerous multidisciplinary and transdisciplinary projects with African-centered foci. Fellowships, communion and networking come in the form of international conferences, symposia and meetings both formal and informal. In order to bridge the divide between the academy and the public sphere, Falola launched the Toyin Falola Interviews (https://www.tfinterviews.com/) in 2020.

It is also important to note that perhaps even more than Wole Soyinka who is also extraordinarily versatile, Falola's transdisciplinary and transcontinental writings are as expansive as Yemoja's waters, the Yoruba goddess of the sea. Sango, the deity of thunder and lightning, and reputed to be the fourth king of the old Oyo Empire, is Falola's guardian spirit just as Ogun, the god of war and iron, presides over Soyinka. Sango was fierce and temperamental, an incorrigible warlord, but in person, Falola is invariably well-mannered and even-tempered and rarely ever, if at all, given to agitated outbursts or displays. And this is why the comparison to Yemoja's pacific expansiveness seems appropriate.

Furthermore, while still contemplating some inherent metaphysical dimensions, arguably, the torrential flow of Falola's intellectual productions do not appear like staccato bursts of thunder *ala* Sango but rather they seem to undulate like calm and steady ocean waves in search of unknown cosmic fulfillment. These particular conceptual origins necessarily speak to the poetics of identity as well as the pragmatics of decolonization in a context still grappling with the after-effects and dilemmas of the colonial encounter.

Ibadan, Falola's home city, rose, in the early nineteenth century, out of the ashes of devastating wars brought on by the jihadist Fulani expansionist drive from the north and the violent internecine conflicts that ravaged Yoruba land during the transatlantic slave trade and British colonial invasion. Renowned for breeding legendary battle generals, Ibadan quickly transformed into a hub of culture and civility that eventually culminated in the establishment of Nigeria's first university in 1948. Falola exemplifies this civil phase of the city which is also renowned as a repository of the finest gems of the Yoruba language, notably in terms of proverbs and philosophical aphorisms.

Some of these laudatory attributes of Yoruba culture are evident in the frequent collective interview sessions Falola hosts to showcase the best minds from the African world such as his royal highness, the late Lamidi Olayiwola Adeyemi, who was the Alaafin (king) of Oyo until 2022. In other to pull off this August event, Falola enlisted the most able purveyors of the Yoruba language.

Communalism, collaboration and community are all key concepts in Falola's practice, vision and philosophy. To a modernist eye and sensibility, a typical—ostensibly rural—Yoruba homestead or hamlet might look rudimentary and perhaps even undeveloped. Ibadan, in particular, seems like an unwieldy amalgam of rust, rusticity and uneven development thickly sprayed with unredeemable red earth. It would be an awful mistake to adopt this superficial view of what appears to be stunted development. Traditional Yoruba communities are usually carefully constructed microcosms woven together by intricacies of hierarchy, language, custom and tradition. Each being within this elaborate social structure is delicately held in place through a web of social relations that continuously affirm the paramountcy of the communal ethos rather than the liberties of the individual. Unfortunately, modernity has sought to subvert and destroy these apparently illustrious sociocultural foundations. Nonetheless, Falola has been largely driven by these communal values and a large part of his work tends to be communal and collaborative in nature.

However, Falola's or even Ibadan's apparent communalism needs to be qualified. As Falola describes it in his inimitable memoir, *A Mouth Sweeter than Salt* (2005), when Ibadan was about to take off as a postwar settlement, its indigenes released two hundred snails in different directions to signify the imminent global pathways and cultural tentacles of the famed city. Accordingly, Falola is a widely traveled indigene with contacts and networks across the globe. Indeed most recently, much of his research has been an engagement with, and an exploration of, the global and cosmopolitan antecedents of the Yoruba beginning from the fifteenth-century apogee of the Oyo Kingdom down to the mass dispersal caused by the transatlantic slave trade which saw the roots and seeds of Yoruba culture planted in Brazil, Barbados, Cuba, Trinidad and Tobago, Colombia and other parts of South

America. A significant part of Falola's work also traces these global trails through discursive reconstructions and contemporary cultural linkages.

Indeed initiatives such as the TFI series are geared toward centering an African voice and perspectives within global civil society thereby collapsing the hegemonic and colonialist center/periphery distinction. Arguably, no other contemporary African scholar has done as much to invalidate the hegemony of this opprobrious distinction through the creation of different platforms and projects of collaborative work.

Africa, just as its teeming peoples, geographies, cultures and histories, is an engaging cauldron of alterity and diversity. We are divided by the most astonishing diversity in terms of indigenous languages not to mention the dominant divisions effected by the Francophone, Anglophone, Arabophone and Lusophone categories. As often noted, it is often easier for postcolonial Africans to communicate with their erstwhile colonial masters than among themselves. The Economic Community of West African States (ECOWAS), the regional economic bloc of the West African region is splintered by the all-too-familiar Anglophone and Francophone dichotomy which creates daunting cultural, linguistic and existential stumbling blocks among nations of the region.

And this is why digital and social media-driven fora like the Toyin Falola Interviews are necessary in order to navigate our differences, fears and mutual suspicion. Colonialism wasn't merely a tussle between colonizer and colonized. It also became, unfortunately, a life-and-death contest among precolonial nationalities and ethnicities. Colonialism created new divisions, articulations of difference and internecine hatreds. These antimonies exist to this day manifested as symptoms of ethnic chauvinism, nationalist bigotry, religious intolerance and xenophobic biases.

Forums such as the Toyin Falola Interviews seek a dispassionate confrontation with this colonial legacy of apprehension of the internal African 'other' which is indeed a manifestation of black anti-black racism, bigotry and intolerance. We have internalized our age-long colonial oppression as hatred of both the self and African other which in fact seems oxymoronic. And this is why the prospect of genocide is always a latent reality.

So far, the Toyin Falola Interviews have hosted royal fathers and leaders, world-renowned academics, prominent social activists and ground-breaking artists. Recent guests on the programme apart from the previously discussed late Alafin of Oyo, Oba Lamidi Adeyemi include, Richard Joseph, emeritus professor at Northwestern University, US, Attahiru Jega, academic, politician and former head of the Independent National Electoral Commission (INEC) of Nigeria, the former president of South Africa, Thabo Mbeki and lastly pioneer of African and African American studies, Afrocentric theory among other pursuits, Molefi Kete Asante.

In these sometimes-heated public exchanges facilitated by Zoom and different social media platforms, Africans from all corners of the world are able to converse across particularist and universalist lines, ventilating their qualms and frustrations on ways to make their lives better. They are also empowered to articulate their ideological positions more clearly. The universalist perspectives of the forum enable ideas to be filtered through considerably less blinkered lenses. On the other hand, the particularist import of various issues endows them with a relevance and urgency we can't simply ignore.

Beyond the particularist and universalist aspects of the series, there is also the powerful Pan-Africanist element in which the ideology gets repurposed for the age of hyper-digitalization, Afrofuturism and trans-humanism. Pan-Africanism is not merely a relic from the colonial era but through a deliberate engagement with the *zeitgeist*, acquires new life and a fresh surge of relevance. Even more, it is a strategic means by which people of African descent engage with the intellectual conundrums of their history and the present times.

Such discursive continuity is necessary to maintain regular cultural and political evolution in an often bewildering age of brutal creative destruction and elimination.

Alas, Pan-Africanism, somewhat refashioned, manages to thrive and provide the psychological bulwark and ideological support many Africans feel are direly lacking in their lives. Indeed, it is still possible to entertain hope via wholesome dialogue, collective reflection and constructive critique even when circumstances turn unremittingly bleak. We have fora such as the Toyin Falola Interviews to thank for encouraging such optimism. Another lesson being offered by the series is that it is possible to dialogue and build enduring bridges over colonially inherited schisms, and in fact, such reconstructions are necessary to ensure varied forms of societal continuity. This is largely a bottom-up and independent approach which makes it all the more promising and interesting.

On Sunday, January 15, 2023, the TFI hosted Omoba Yemisi Shyllon, one of Nigeria's most fascinating art collectors whose presentation portrays the vagaries of maintaining his hobby in a postcolonial context. Art collecting in large parts of Africa is saddled with the usual colonialist apprehensions and prejudices and is often viewed with suspicion by those beholden to both the Islamic and Christian faiths which discourage the worldly adoration of 'graven images'. These ingrained religious presuppositions have done much to undermine the unfurling of the creative spirit in significant parts of the continent. Shyllon, who is an engineer, lawyer, stockbroker, art merchant, and management consultant precariously maintains a location between tradition and modernity in which he courageously struggles to privilege the former in the face of considerable public consternation and dismay. He has established the Prince Yemisi Shyllon Museum which hosts the largest private collection of sculptures by the globally renowned Yoruba artist, Lamidi Olonade Fakeye of the illustrious Fakeye wood carving dynasty of Ila-Orangun, western Nigeria. Apart from publishing a co-authored book on Lamidi, Shyllon also has a sizable gathering of Bisi Fakeye's (Lamidi's nephew) works.

In hosting events such as this, some of the conceptual tensions in Falola's work become more evident; the unending tussles between historical memory and collective amnesia, communalist worldviews and strident individualism, and quaint folk epistemologies and solitary genius. Indeed, Falola has not only been able to strike the right balance between these seemingly irreconcilable dichotomies but also has managed to nurture innumerable interpersonal relationships over diverse nations and regions for a nurturing social existence in an ultra-digital age.

Endnotes

1 Introduction, *Sango in Africa and the Diaspora*, eds. Joel E. Tishken, Toyin Falola and Akintunde Akinyemi, Indiana University Press, Bloomington and Indianapolis, 2009, p. 1.
2 Ibid. 2.
3 Ibid.

UNFINISHED BUSINESS

I remember the night in 2014, after a delicious bout of carousing, when discussions casually devolved upon the possibilities of producing a book on Falola's vast corpus. I was swamped with the regular academic duties of teaching, marking scripts and mentoring amid other sundry administrative worries. But still, it seemed a viable endeavor for the future.

In between, Falola included me in other pivotal projects; a Nelson Mandela collaborative volume he edited for Carolina Academic Press in 2014; The imaginatively conceived and executed Indiana University Press released *Encyclopedia of the Yoruba* in 2016; The lavish *Palgrave Macmillan Handbook of African Philosophy* in 2017; The *Palgrave Macmillan Handbook of African Social Ethics* in 2020 being the major ones. Of course, there were other numerous occasions to collaborate. I attended most of the inspiring Toyin Falola Interview Series in which he and other panelists grilled distinguished African leaders and scholars on various continental matters. Falola's life and work are invariably filled with an endless stream of activities, projects and events. But in his personal relations, one never senses the frenetic pace of those prolific activities. He is usually calm and solicitous in conversation and in my case, he listened far more than he shared his views. He always seemed to want to know what I thought about a wide range of issues and ideas. His publishers and editors would solicit blurbs for his unending array of book projects. He would ask for opinions on book proposals he was working on. He endlessly shared his equally prodigious articles in popular media for comments and reactions. I was overawed by his productivity and equanimity.

Meanwhile, my book project on his outstanding corpus stuttered and puttered. When I wasn't battling other cares and commitments, I was tearing out my hair about finding a suitable conceptual and theoretical approach to a project that threatened to drown me on account of its innate shapelessness and vastness. And then my philosophical training asserted itself. Perhaps it wasn't judicious to approach Falola's work from the point of view of its stupendous prodigality. Better to execute the project from a purely conceptual and theoretical standpoint in which certain recurrent motifs are addressed to extrapolate a few foundational elements of his corpus which can then serve as a guide for future scholarship and reflections. Once I seized upon this reckoning, my intellectual challenge became considerably more endurable. And then the urgency to complete the text receded.

The shape of this essay was found to be formed after this epiphanic realization. I promptly approached Falola for an interview to accompany this essay. I sent him 20 questions on his life, work and reflections. I hadn't anticipated the prolixity of his responses. It was far more than I would have ever imagined. In seeking to write a monograph on Falola's expansive scholarship, he himself had written the book I was having trouble writing, and he wrote it better than I could have ever written it. All I had to do was to provide a context for the writing, and the circumstances that accompanied its gestation, evolution and consummation.

This is essentially what this introduction seeks to do. Falola compels a reflection on various traditions of African intellectual culture that privilege the *logos*, orality and communal ethos. Falola does not actually recommend this approach in this exchange but much of the implications derived from his work suggest it. He does not approach scholarship with a literal mind, to deliver the book *ala* Karl Marx, James Joyce or Frantz Fanon. He does not attempt to compose an opus that would encapsulate life, knowledge and meaning in a single, intense, encyclopedic sweep even if there are traces of these in his numerous books. Instead, his texts work as a series of journeys, diversions and caesuras, shattered prisms of wisdom, perspectives and *volte faces*, attesting to the multiplicity of existence, truth, perfection, foibles and death. Even more, these ever-shifting prisms are not serrated, linked by conceptual symmetries and conjunctions since the underlying energies simply aren't assembled in that manner.

This text, hopefully, captures Falola's generous mind and voice at various stages of his life and career among the Yoruba to the globalized personal and institutional networks, interactions and production he has diligently developed and which have subsequently transformed into him into a pivotal figure of the contemporary intellectual world. In these remarkable discussions, certain key concepts and terminologies are frequently implied explicitly, or at least, implicitly; communalism, reciprocity, transdisciplinarity, interculturality, and various iterations of cosmopolitanism.

BIBLIOGRAPHY

Abimbola, W. (1977) *Àwọn Ojú Odù Mẹ́rẹ̀ẹ̀rindínlógún*, London: Oxford University Press.

———. (1998) "The Bag of Wisdom:Ọ̀ṣun and the Origins of the ifá Divination." In *Ọ̀ṣiun Across the Waters: A Yorùbá Goddess in Africa and the Americas*, eds. Joseph M. Murphy and Mei Mei Sanford, 141–54. Bloomington: Indiana University Press.

———. (1976) *Ifá: An Exposition of Ifá Literary Corpus*, Ibadan, Nigeria: Oxford University Press.

———. (1973) *Ìjìnlẹ̀ Ohun Ẹnu ifá*, Glasgow: Collins.

———. (1975) "Introduction" In *Yorùbá Oral Tradition, Poetry in Music, Dance and Drama*, ed. Wande Abimbola, II–48. Ilẹ-ifẹ̀, Nigeria: Department of African Languages and Literature, University of Ifẹ̀.

———. (1981) *Proceedings of the First World Conference on Òrìṣà Tradition*. Ilé-ifẹ́, Nigeria: Ọbáfẹ́mi Awolọ́wọ́ University.

———. (1976–77) "The Yorùbá Traditional Religion in Brazil: Problems and Prospects." In *Seminar Series*, Number I.I, ed. O. Oyelaran, I–64. Ilé-ifẹ̀, Nigeria: Department of African Languages and Literatures, University of Ife.

Abiodun, R. "Ifa Art Objects: An Interpretation based on Oral Tradition. "In *Yorùbá Oral Tradition; Poetry in Music, Dance and Drama*, ed. Wande Abimbola, 421–66. Ilé-ifẹ̀, Nigeria: Department of African Languages and Literature, University of Ifẹ̀, 1975.

Abraham, R. C. (1962) *Dictionary of Modern Yoruba*, London: Hodder and Stoughton. 1962.

Addie, O. O. (1990) "Colour Symbolism, with Special Reference to Sango Shrine in Ibadan" Unpublished B.A long essay, Ọbáfẹ́mi Awolọ́wọ́ University, Ile-ifẹ̀.

Adebisi, S. (1986) "Shrine Painting in Ilé-ifẹ̀. "Unpublished B.A. long essay, Ọbáfẹ́mi Awolọ́wọ́ University, Ilé-Ifẹ̀, 1986.

Adedeji, J. A. (1966) "The Place of Drama in Yorùbá Religious Observance" *Odu* 3; 88–94.

Adegbile, I. O. (1999) *Yorùbá Names and Their Meanings plus Proverbs with English Translations*, Ibadan, Nigeria: Taa Printing and Publishing.

Adelugba, D. (1981) "Trance and Theatre; the Nigerian Experience." In *Drama and Theatre in Nigeria: A Critical Source Book*, ed. Yemi Ogunbiyi, 203–18. Lagos: Nigeria Magazine.

Adeoye, C. L. (1979) *Àṣà ati Ìṣe Yorùbá*, Oxford: Oxford University Press.

———. (1985) *Ìgbàgbọ́ ati Èṣìn Yorùbá (Yorùbá religious belief systems)*, Ibadan, Nigeria: Evans Brothers Nigerian Publishers.

Adewoye, O. (1987). Proverbs as Vehicle of Juristic Thought Among the Yoruba. *Obafemi University Law Journal*, 3, 1–17.

Afolabi, N. (2001) "Beyond the Curtains: Unveiling Afro-Brazilian Women Writers." *Research in African Literatures* 32, no. 4 (Winter 2001): 117–35.

Afolayan, F. (2000) "Kingdoms of West Africa: Benin, Ọ̀yọ́ Asante. "In *Africa: vol. I, African History Before 1885*, ed. Toyin Falola, 161–89. Durham, NC: Carolina Academic Press.

Ahye, M. (1981) "Ṣàngó in Trinidad: Its Survival and Retention. "In *Proceedings of the First World Conference on Òrìṣà Tradition*, ed. Wande Abimbola, 130–91. Ilé-ifẹ̀, Nigeria: University of Ife, June 1–7.

Aiyejina, F., and Rawle G. (1999) "Òrìṣà (Òrìṣhà) Tradition in Trinidad." Paper presented at the Ninth International Orisa Congress. Port of Spain, Trinidad.

Ajayi, J. F. A. (1974) "The Aftermath of the Fall of Ọyọ." In *History of West Africa*, eds. J.F Ade Ajayi and Micheal Crowder, 129–66. London: Longman.

———. (2000) "Development is about People." In *Humanity in Context*, ed. Ayo Banjo, 1–31. Ibadan, Nigeria: Nigeria Academy of Letters.

Ajuwon, B. (1981) "Ogun: premus Inter Pares." In *Proceedings of the First World Conference on Orisa Tradition*, ed. Wande Abimbola, 425–50. Ilé-ifẹ̀, Nigeria: Obafemi, Awolowo University.

Akanmu A. (1999) "Kose-e-mani: Idealism and Contradiction in the Yoruba View of Money." In *Credit, Currencies and Culture African Financial Institutions in Historical Perspective*, eds. Endre Stiansen and Jane Guyer, 146–74. Uppsala: Nordiska Afrika Institutet.

Akinjogbin, I.A. (1972) "The Expansion of Ọyọ and the Rise of Dahomey, 1600-1800." In *The History of West Africa*, vol 1. New York; Columbia University Press.

Akinjogbin, A.I (2002) *Milestones and Concepts in Yoruba History and Culture: A Key to Understanding Yoruba History*, Ibadan: Olu-Akin Publishers.

Akinjogbin A.I (1976) "The Ebi System Reconsidered," *Department of History Seminar Series*, 978–1979, University of Ife: Ilé-ifẹ̀: Kosalabaro Press, 16.

Akinyemi, A. (2004) *Yorùbá Royal Poetry: A Socio-historical Exposition and Annotated Translation*. Bayreuth African Studies Series (BASS), number 71. Bayreuth, Germany: University of Bayreuth.

Alade, C.A. "Aspects of Yoruba Culture in the Diaspora. 'In Culture in the Diaspora'." In *Culture and Society in Yorùbá Land*, eds. Deji Ogunremi and Biodun Adediran, 203–11.

Abimbola, Wande. (1968) *Ijinle Ohun Enu Ifa*, 1, Glasgow, UK: Aim Press.

———. (1995) "Notes on Orisha Cults in the Ekiti Yoruba Highlands." *Cahiers d'Études africaines* 35, nos. 138–39: 369–401.

Andrew A. (1987) "Historiography of Yoruba Myth," *History in Africa* 14.

Atanda, J. A. (1980) *An Introduction to Yorùbá History Ibadan*, Nigeria: Ibadan University Press.

———. (1973) *The New Ọ̀yọ́ Empire*, London: Longmans.

Awe, B. (1973) "Militarism and Economic Developments in Nineteenth Century Yorùbá Country: The Ibadan Example." *Journal of African History* 14, No. 1: 65–77.

Aweda, S. (2002) (*Ẹẹ̀rìndínlógún* priest). Interview conducted by the author at Alubàtá Compound Èkọsín, Odò-Ọ̀tin Local Government, Ọsun State, Nigeria, 2002–2003.

Awolalu, J. O. (2001) *Yorùbá Beliefs and Sacrificial Rites (1970)*, Brooklyn: Athelia Henrietta Press.

Awolalu, J. O., & Awolalu, J. O. (1979). *Yoruba Beliefs and Sacrificial Rites*, Longman.

Ayodeji O. (1999) "Introduction." In *Northeast Yorubaland: Studies in the History and Culture of a Frontier Zone*. eds. Ayodeji Olukoju, Z.O. Apata, and Olayemi Akinwumi, Ibadan: Rex Charles, 1.

Babalola, S.A. (1966) *Content and Form of Yorùbá Ìjálú*. London: Oxford University Press.

Babayemi, S.O. (1973) "Bẹẹrẹ Festival in Ọ̀yọ́" *Journal of Historical Society of Nigeria* 7, no 1, 121–23.

Babayemi, S. (1979) "The Fall and Rise of Ọ̀yọ́ 1760–1905." Ph.D. diss, University of Birmingham.

———. (1976) "The Myths of Oranyan in Yoruba Historiography." M.A. thesis, University of Birmingham.

Badejo, D. L. (1982) *Field Notes*, Nigeria.

———. (2004) "Methodologies in Yoruba Oral Historiographies and Aesthetics." In *Writing African History*, ed. John Edward Philips, 348–73. Rochester, N.Y: University of Rochester Press.

Balderson, D., Mike G., and Ana M. La (2002) *The Encyclopedia of Contemporary Latin American and Caribbean Cultures*, New York: Routledge, 2002.

Bamidele, L. (2003) "Sango Myth and Its Challenges in Science, Art and Religion." In *IBA: Essays on African Literature in Honour of Oyin Ogunba*, eds. W. Ogundele and O. Adeoti, 178–86. Ilé-ifẹ̀, Nigeria: Obafemi Awolowo University Press.

Barber, Karin, (1989) "Como o homen cria Deus na África Ocidental: atitudes dos Yoruba Para com o Orisa." In *Meu Sinal esta no teu corpo*, ed. C. E. Moura, 142-73. Sao Paulo, Brazil: EDICON-EDUSP.

———. (1981) "How Man makes God in West African: Yoruba Attitudes towards the Òrìsà." *Africa* 51, no. 3: 724–45.

———. (1979) "Oríkì in Òkukù: Relationship between Verbal and Social Structures." Ph.D. diss., University of Ife.

———. (1984) "Yorùbá Oriki and Deconstructive Criticism." *Research in African Literature* 15, no. 4; 501–29.

Barnes, S. T. (1989) *Africa's Ogun: Old World and New*, Bloomington: Indiana University Press.

Bascom, W. (1973) *African Art in Cultural Perspective: An Introduction*, New York: W. W. Norton.

———. (1969) *Ifá Divination: Communication Between Gods and Men in West African*, Bloomington; Indiana University Press.

———. (1972) *Shàngó in the New World*, Austin: African and Afro-American Research Institute, University of Texas at Austin.

———. (1980) *Sixteen Cowries: Yoruba Divination from Africa to the New World*, Bloomington: Indiana University Press, 1980.

Bastide, Roger. (1978) *Images du nor-deste mystique en noir et blanc (1945)*, Paris: Pandora Editions.

———. (1986) *Sociologia de la Religion (Les religious africaines au Bresil) (1960)*, Gijón, Spain: Ediciones jucar.

Baudin, P. (1884) *Fetichism and Fetich Worshippers*, New York: Benziger Bros.

Beier, U. (1994) *The Return of Shàngó: The Theater of Duro Ladipo*, Bayreuth, Germany: University of Bayreuth.

———. (1959) *A Year of Sacred Festivals in One Yorùbá Town*, Lagos: Nigeria Magazine.

———. (1959) A Year of Sacred Festivals in One Yorùbá Town (ẸDẸ): *Nigeria Magazine (Special* Production), 3rd ed, 9, 72–79.

———. (1980) *Yorùbá Myths*, Cambridge: Cambridge University Press.

———. (1960) "Yorùbá Wall Paintings" *ODU: Journal of Yorùbá and Edo Related Studies* 8: 36–9.

Benkomo, J. (2000)"Crafting the Sacred Batá Drums." In *Afro-Cuban Voices: On Race and Identity in Contemporary Cuba*, eds. Pedro Pérez Sarduy and Jean Stubbs, 140–46. Gainesville: University Press of Florida.

Bettelheim, J. (2001) *Cuban Festivals: A Century of Afro-Cuban Culture*, Princeton, N.J: Markus Wiener Publishers.
Bewaji, J.A.I (1992) "A Critical Analysis of the Philosophical Status of Yoruba Ifa Literary Corpus," *Wiener Reihe*,6, 142–155.
Biobaku, S. O. (1975) *The Ègbá and Their Neighbors 1842–1872*, Oxford: Oxford University Press.
Birth, K. (1999) *Any Time is Trinidad Time: Social meanings and Temporal Consciousness*, Gainesville: University Press of Florida.
Bolaji I. E. (1962) *Olodumare: God in Yoruba Belief*, London: Longman.
Bomfim, M. E. d. (1940). "Os Ministros de Xango." In *O Negro no Brasil: trabalhos apresentados ao 2 congresso Afro-Brasileiro, Bahia 1937*, 233–36. Rio de Janeiro: Civiliacao Brasileira.
Borghero, Francesco. (1865) *Jounal de Francesco Borghero, premier missionnaire du Dahomey (1861–1865)*, eds. Renzo Mandirolaa and Yves Morel. Paris: Karthala.
Bourguignon, E. "Relativism amd Ambivalence in the Work of M.J. Herskovits." *Ethos*, 1 (200); 103–14.
Bowen, R. T.J. (1858) *A Grammar and Dictionary of Yoruba Language*, Washington D.C: Smithsonian Institution.
Braga, J. (1992) *Ancestralidade Afro-Brasileira; o culto de babá egun*, Salvador, Brazil: CEAO Ianamá.
———. (1995) *Na Gamela do Feitico, repressao e Resistencia nos Candombles da Bahia*, Salvador, Brazil: EDUFBA.
Brain, R. A. (1980) *Society in Africa*, New York: Longman group.
Brereton, B. (1979) *Race Relations in Colonial Trinidad, 1870–1900*, New York; Cambridge University Press.
Browker, John, ed. (1997) *The Oxford Dictionary of World Religions*, New York; Oxford University Press.
Brown, D. H. (2003) *Santeria Enthroned: Art, Ritual, and Innovation in an Afro-Cuban Religion*, Chicago: University of Chicago Press.
Burket, W. (1985) *Greek Religion*. Trans. John Raffan. Cambridge, MA.: Harvard University Press.
Cabrera, L. (1954) *El Monte*, Miami, FL.: Ediciones Universal, 1983.
Campbell, V.B. (1989) "Comparative Study of Selected Shrine Paintings in Ilé-Ifẹ̀ and Ilésà "Unpublished M.F.A. diss., Ọbáfẹ́mi Awolọ́wọ́ University, Ilé Ifẹ̀.
———. (1992) "Continuity and Change in Yorùbá Shrine Painting Tradition." *Kurio Africana: Journal of Art and Criticism* 1, no. 2; 110–23.
———. (1995) "Images and Power in Sixteen Yoruba Sacred Paintings." Ife: *Annuals of the Institute of Cultural Studies*: 25–38.
Canizares, B. R. (2000) *Shango: Santeria and the Òrìshà of Thunder*, Plainview, N.Y.: Original Publication.
Capone, S. (1999) *La quete de L'Afrique dans le candomblé. Pouvoir et tradition au Brésil*, Paris: Karthala.
Carneiro, E. (1984) *Candomblés da Bahia*, Salvador, Brazil: Ediouro.
Carroll, K. with foreword by William F. (1967) *Yorùbá Religious Carving: Pagan and Christian Sculpture in Nigeria and Dahomey*, London: Geoffrey Chapman.
Castor, N. (1999) "Virtual Community: The Òrìṣà Tradition in the New World and Cyberspace." Paper Presented at the Ninth International Òrìṣà Conference, Port of Spain, Trinidad.

Catherine M. (1997) "Feminism, Marxism, Method, and the State: An Agenda for Theory." In *Feminist Social Thought: A Reader,* ed. D.T. Meyers. New York: Routledge.
Catholic Community Forum. (2005) "Patron Saints Index: Saint Barbara." N.D. (Accessed Jan 30, 2005) http://www.catholic-forum.com/saints/saintbo.
Clapperton, H. (2005) *Hugh Clapperton into the Interior of Africa; Records of the Second Expedition, 1825–1827.* eds. Jamie Bruce Lockhart and Paul. Love joy, Boston: Brill.
Clake, K. M. (2004) *Mapping Yoruba Network: Power and Agency in the Making of Transnational Communities,* Durham, N.C.: Duke University Press.
Comaroff, J. and John L. C. (2004) *Millennial Capitalism and the Culture of Neoliberalism,* Durham, N.C: Duke University Press.
Conner, R. P., and David H. S. (2004) *Queering Creole Spiritual Traditions: Lesbian, Gay, Bisexual and Transgender Participation in African Inspired Traditions in the Americas,* New York: Harrington Park Press.
Courlander, H. (1973) *Tales of Yorùbá Gods and Heroes: Myths, Legend and heroic Tales of the Yorùbá People of West Africa,* New York: Crown Publishers.
———. (1975) *A Treasury of African Folklore,* New York: Crown.
Daramola O. and Jeje A. (1970) *Asa ati Awon Orisa Ile Yoruba,* Ibadan: Onibonoje Press, 160.
Daramola, O. and Jeje, A. (1967) *Àwọn Àṣà àti Òrìṣà ilẹ̀ Yorùbá,* Ibadan, Nigeria; Onibonoje Press.
Diamini, I. (1985) *Speaking for Ourselves,* Braamfontein, South Africa: Institute for Contextual Theology.
———. (1986) "Zionist Churches from the Perspective of a Zionist leader." In *Religion Alive,* ed. G. C. Oosthuizen, 209–10. Johannesburg: Hodder and Stoughton.
Drewal H. J. (1980) *African Artistry: Technique and Aesthetics in Yorùbá Sculpture,* Atlanta: High Museum of Art.
Drewel, H. J. and John P. III, with Rowland A. (1989) *Yorùbá: Nine Centuries of African Art and Thought,* New York; Center for African Art in association with harry n. Abrahams.
Drewal, M. T. (1992) *Yorùbá Ritual: Performers, Play, Agency,* Bloomington: Indiana University Press.
Dwyer, K. (1982) *Moroccan Dialogues: Anthropology in Question,* Baltimore, MD: Johns Hopkins University Press.
Egonwa, D. O. (1995) "Patterns and Trends of stylistic Development in Contemporary Nigerian Art," *Kurio Africana; Journal of Art and Criticism* 2 (I): 1–15.
Ehret, C. (2002) *The Civilizations of Africa; a History of 1800,* Charlottesville; University Press of Virginia.
Ellis, A. B. (1970) *The Yorùbá Speaking Peoples of the Slave Coast of West Africa: Their Religion, Manners, Customs, Laws, Language, etc. (1894),* Oosterhout, Netherlands, Anthropological Publications.
Eltis, D. (2004) "The Diaspora of Yorùbá Speakers, 1650-1865: Dimensions and Implications. "In *In the Yoruba Diaspora in the Atlantic World,* eds. Toyin Falola and Matt Childs, 17–39. Bloomington: Indiana University Press.
Euba, A. (1990) *Yoruba Drumming: The Dùndún Tradition,* Bayreuth, Germany: African Studies Series.
Fadipe, N. A. (1991) *The Sociology of the Yorùbá,* Ibadan, Nigeria: Ibadan University Press, 1970 (original year of publication).
Fakeye, L. O., Haight M. B. and Curl D.. , (1996) *A Retrospective Exhibition and Autobiography,* Holland, Mich: De Pree Art Center and Gallery.

Fakinlede, K. J. (2003). "Yoruba: Modern Practical Dictionary Yoruba-English." *English-Yorùbá*, New York: Hippocrene Books.
Falola, Toyin. (1999). *Yoruba Gurus: Indigenous Production of Knowledge in Africa*, Africa World Press.
Falola, Toyin. and Matt D. C. (2004) *The Yoruba Diaspora in the Atlantic World*, Bloomington: Indiana University Press.
Falola, Toyin. and Ann G. (2005) *Òrìṣà: Yorùbá Gods and Spiritual Identity in Africa and the Diaspora*, Trenton: Africa World Press.
Falola, Toyin. (2013) *A Mouth Sweeter than Salt: An African Memoir*, Bookcraft: Ibadan, Nigeria.
Fartunsin, A. K (1992) *Yorùbá Pottery*, Lagos: National Commission for Museums and Monuments.
Ferreira, Pai Euclides Menezes (2003) Interview with Luis Nicolau Parés. June 25, 2003.
Folanrami, S. (2002) "The Importance of Oríkí in Yorùbá Mural Art." *Ijele Art e-Journal of the African World* 2, no. 4. Available at www.africaresource.com
———. (1995) "Òrìṣá Pópó Shrine Painting in Ògbómọ̀ṣọ́." Unpublished B.A. long essay, Ọbáfẹ́mi Awólọ́wò University, Ile Ife.
———. (2000) "Ọ̀yọ Palace Mural; Unpublished M.F.A. thesis, Ọbáfẹ́mi Awólọ́wò University, Ile Ife.
———. (2002) "Ọ̀yọ Palace Mural; a Symbolic Communications with Symbols." *Journal of Art and Ideas* 4: 93–105.
Font, M. A. (2005) "Introduction: The Intellectual Legacy of Fernando Ortiz." In *Cuban Counterpoints: The Legacy of Fernando Ortiz*, ed. Mauricio A. Font, 1–27. Baltimore, MD: Lexington Books.
Forbes, F. E. (1851) *Dahomey and the Dahomeans*. 2 vols. London: Longman, Brown, Green, and Longmans.
Fosu, K. (1986) *20th Century Art of Africa*. Vol 1. Zaria, Nigeria: Gaskiya Corporation.
Foucault, M. (1991) "Governmentality." In *The Foucault Effect: Studies in Governmentality*, eds. G. Burchell, C. Gordon, and P. Miller, 87–104. London: Harvester Wheatsheaf.
Fraginals, M. M. (1976) *The Sugarmill: The Socioeconomic Complex of Sugar in Cuba, 1760–1860*. Trans. Cedric Belfrage. New York: Monthly Review Press.
Fredrick, A. (1995) Praeger Publisher, 1963; rev and enlarged ed, London: Longman.
Frobenius, L. (1968) *The Voice of Africa: Being an Account of the Travels of the German Inner African Exploration Expedition in the Years 1910-1912*. Trans Rudolf Blind, 2 vol London: Hutchinson, 1913; Benjamin Bloom.
Gibbons, R. (1999) "Introduction and Welcome." *Paper Presented at the Ninth International Òrìṣà Congress, Port of Spain, Trinidad*.
Glazier, S. D. (1991) *Marching' The Pilgrim Home: A Study of the Spiritual Baptists of Trinidad*, Salem, Wisc: Sheffield.
———. (1995) "New World African Ritual: Genuine and Spurious." *Journal for the Scientific Study of Religion* 35, no 4, 420–31.
———. (1998) "The Religious Mosaic: Playful Celebration in Trinidadian Shàngó." *Play and Culture* 1, 216–35.
———. (1993) "Responding to the Anthropologist: When the Spiritual Baptists of Trinidad Read What I Write about Them." In *When They Read What We Write: The Politics of Ethnography*, ed. Caroline B. Brettell, 37–48. Westport, CT: Bergin and Garvey.
———. (2001) ed. *Encyclopedia of African and African-American Religious*, New York Bergin and Garvey.

Gleason, J. (1971) *Òrìshà: The Gods of Yorùba Land*, New York: Atheneum.
Gotrick, K. (1984) *Apidán Theatre and Modern Drama*, Stockholm: Almovist and Wiksell International.
Goveia, E. (1960) "The West Indian Slave Laws of the Eighteenth Century." *Revista de Ciencias Sociales* 4, 75–105.
Greenfield, S. M, and Andre D. (2002) *Reinventing Religions: Syncretism and Transformation in Africa and the Americas*, New York: Rowman and Littlefield.
Grimes, R. (1994) *Beginnings in Ritual Studies*, Columbia: University of South Carolina Press.
Hall, G. M. (1971) *Social Control in Slave Plantation Societies: A Comparison of St, Domingue and Cuba*, Baltimore, MD: Johns Hopkins Press.
Hancock, F. (1971) "West Africa and the Atlantic Creoles." In *The English Language in West Africa*, eds. John J. Spencer: London: Longman.
Hardt, M. and Antonio N. (2000) *Empire Cambridge*, MA: Harvard University Press.
Hart H. L. A. (1957) "Positivism and the Separation of Laws and Morals," *Harvard Law Review*, 71, 57–58.
Harry G. L. (2000) "Leaving the United States: The Black Nationalist Themes of Orisha-Vodu," *Journal of Black Studies* 31, No 2, 174-76, 185.
Hartnoll, P. (1998) *The Theatre: A Concise History*, 3rd ed. New York: Thames and Hudson.
Hastrup, K. (1992) "Writing Ethnography: State of the Art." In *Anthropology and Autobiography*, eds. J. Okley and H. Callaway, 116–33. New York: Routledge.
Henry, F. (2001) "The Òrìshà (Shàngó) Movement in Trinidad." In *Encyclopedia of African and African-American Religious*, ed. Stephen D. Glazier, 221–23. New York: Routledge.
———. (2003) *Reclaiming Africans Religious in Trinidad: The Socio-Political Legitimization of the Òrìshà and Spiritual Baptist Faiths*, Mona, Jamaica: University of the West Indies Press.
Hernandez-Reguant, A. (2022) "Radio Taino and the Globalization of the Cuban Culture Industries." Ph.D. diss., University of Chicago.
Herbert, E. W. (1993) *Iron, Genders and Power, Rituals of Transformation in African Societies*, Bloomington: Indiana University Press.
Herskovits, M. J. (1947) *Culture Dynamics*, New York: Alfred A. Knopf.
Herskovits, M. J., and Frances H. (1947) *Trinidad Village*, New York: Alfred A. Knopf.
Hethersett, A. L. (1941) *Ìwé Kíkà Èkẹrin Lí Èdè Yorùbá*, Lagos, Nigeria: Church Missionary Society.
Higginbotham, J. and River H. (2002) *Paganism: An Introduction to Earth-Centered Religious*, St. Paul, MN: Llewellyn Publications.
Horn, A. (1981) "Ritual, Drama and the Theatrical: The Case of Bori Spirit Medium." In *Drama and Theatre in Nigeria: A Critical Source Book*, ed. Yemi Ognbiyi, 181–202. Lagos: Nigeria Magazine.
Horton, R. "African Conversion." *Africa* 41 9197: 85-108.
Houk, James T. (1995) *Spirits, Blood and Drums: The Òrìshà Religion in Trinidad*, Philadelphia: Temple University Press.
Hucks, Tracey E. (2001) "Trinidad, Africa-Derived Religions." In *Encyclopedia of African and African American Religious*, ed. Stephen D. Glazier, 338–43. New York: Routledge.
Hugh, T. (1964) *Rise of Christian Europe*, London: Thames and Hudson, 9.
Hugh, K. (1983) "Wisdom of the Tribe: Why Proverbs Are Better than Aphorisms." *Haper's, May 6, 1983, 84*.
Ibadan, Apter, A. (1992) *Black Critics and Kings: The Hermeneutics of Power in Yoruba Society*, Chicago: University of Chicago Press.
Idowu, E. B. (1962) *Olódùmarè: God in Yorùbá Belief*, London: Longman.

Idowu W. (2006) "Against the Skeptical Argument and the Absence Thesis: African Jurisprudence and the Challenge of Positivist Historiography," *Journal of Philosophy, Science and Law*, 6, 2006, 34–48.

Idowu W. (2006) "African Jurisprudence and Reconciliation Theory of Law," *Cambrian Law Review*, 37, 1–16.

Idowu W. (2009) "Eurocentrism and Separability-Inseparability Debates: Challenges from African Cultural Jurisprudence," *Journal of Pan-African Studies*, 2(9) 123–50.

Idowu, W. (2005). Law, morality and the African cultural heritage: the jurisprudential significance of the Ogboni institution. *Nordic Journal of African Studies*, 14(2), 18.

Ifaoogun, A. B. (2001). *(Ifa Priest). Interview conducted by the author in Ìlobùu M*, Ọṣun State, Nigeria.

Isola, Akinwumi. (2000). "Èdè-Àìyedè tí ó rọ orírun Ṣàngo." In *O Pegedé: Àkojọpọ̀ Àwọn Àròkọ Akadá fún yíyònbóỌ̀jògbọ́n Adébóyè Babalọlà*, ed. O Olutoye, 113–19. Ikeja, Nigeria: Longman Nigeria Plc.

———. (1984). "The Living Power of Ṣàngó." *Proceedings of the First World Conference on Òrìṣà Tradition*, ed. Wande Abimbola, 338–46. Held at the University of Ife, Ile-Ife, Nigeria, June 1–7.

———."Orin Etíyẹrí." Unpublished Paper.

———. (1991). "Religious Politics and the Myth of Ṣango." In *African Traditional Religion in Contemporary Society*, ed. Jacob K. Olupona, 93–99. New York: Paragon.

———. (1975). "The Rhythm of Ṣàngó Pípè." In *Yoruba Oral Tradition: Poetry in Music, Dance and Drama*, ed. Wande Abimbola, 76–93. Ile-Ife, Nigeria: Department of African Languages and Literature, University of Ife.

———. (1973). Ṣàngó-Pípè, One type of Yoruba Oral Poetry. M.A. thesis, University of Lagos.

———. (1977). Yorùbá Beliefs about Ṣàngó as a Deity. *Orita: Ibadan Journal of Religious Studies* II, no. 2, 100–20.

Itacy, J. O. (1989). *Orixas e voduns nos terreiros de Mina*, Sao luis, Brazil; VCR Producoes e Publicidades.

Jackson, M. (2003) *Minima Ethnographica: Inter-subjectivity and the Anthropological Project*, Chicago; University Press.

Jane S. (1995) "Feminist Jurisprudence," In *Contemporary Feminist Theory*, eds. Stevi Jackson and Jackie Jones, Edinburgh: Edinburgh University Press.

John F. (1980). *Natural Law and Natural Rights*, Oxford: Clarendon Press, 359–60.

Johnson, S. (1966). *The History of the Yorùbás: From earliest times to the Beginning of the British Protectorate* (1921), O. Johnson, ed. London: Routledge and Kegan Paul, Lagos: C.S.S; 1960, 1976.

Joseph M. M. and Mei-Mei S. (2001). *Osun across the Waters*, 1–6, Bloomington, IN: Indiana University Press.

Joseph O. (1987) *The Gullah: Rice, Slavery, and the Sierra Leone-America Connection (Pamphlet)*, Freetown, Sierra Leone: USIS.

Judith G. (1971) *Orisha: The Gods of Yorubaland*, New York: Atheneum.

Kerenyi, C. (2000) *The Gods of the Greeks (1951)*, London: Thames and Hudson.

Kirsch, J. (2004) *God against the gods: The History of the war between Monotheism and Polytheism*, New York: Vikings Compass.

Klass, M. (1991) When God Can Do Anything; Belief Systems in Collision. *Anthropology of Consciousness* 2: 3–34.

Klaus F. (1996). "Farewell to Legal Positivism." In *The Autonomy of Law: Essays on Legal Positivism*, ed. R.P. George, Oxford: Clarendon Press.

BIBLIOGRAPHY

Kinght, F. (1970) *Slave Society in Cuba during the Nineteenth Century*, Madison: University of Wisconsin Press.
Koch, K.F. (1974) *War and Peace in Jalemo*, Cambridge, MA: Harvard University Press.
Kwame A. (1992) *In My Father's House: Africa in the Philosophy of Culture*, London: Methuen, 144.
Kwame G. (1997). *Tradition and Modernity a Philosophical Reflection on the African Experience*, New York: Oxford University Press, 242.
Lacerda, M. B. (1996) "Yorùbá Drums from Benin, West Africa." In *Yorùbá Drums from Benin, West Africa*. CD liner notes. Washington, D.C.: Smithsonian Folksways Recordings.
Ladipo, D. (1972) *Ọba Kòso (The King Did Not Hang)*. Ibadan, Nigeria: Macmillan Nigeria, 1970; Institute of African Studies at the University of Ibadan.
Ladipo, P. A. (1992) Ṣàngó Shrine Painting in Ẹdẹ. Unpublished B.A. long essay, Ọbáfẹ́mi Awólọ́wọ̀ University, Ilé-Ifẹ̀.
Landes, R. (1947) *City of Women*, Albuquerque: University of New Mexico Press.
Lanternari, V. (1963) *Religious of the Oppressed*, New York: Alfred A. Knopf.
Larsen S., *Writer A. and His Gods (1983) A Study of the Importance of Yoruba Myths and Religious Ideas to the Writing of Wole Soyinka*, Stockholm: University of Stockholm Press.
Law, R. (1997) Ethnicity and the Slave Trade: "Lucumi" and 'Nago' as Ethnonyms in West Africa. *History in Africa* 24, 205–19.
———. (1970) *The Ọ̀yọ́ Empire, c 1600-1836: A West Africa Imperialism in the Era of the Atlantic Slave Trade*, Oxford; Clarendon Press, .
Lépine, C. (1982) "Análise Formal do panteao nago." In *Bandeira de Alaira: out ros escritos sobre a religiao dos orixas*, ed. C.E.M de Moura, 13–70. Sao Paulo, Brazil: NobeL.
Leuzinger, E. (1976) *The Art of Black Africa*, London: Cassel and Collier Macmillan Publishers.
Lewis, I.M. (1971) *Ecstatic Religion*, Middlesex, England: Penguin Books.
Lima, M. H. (2005) "Introduction." In *Mulheres Escrevendo: Uma Antologia Bilingue de Escritoras Afro-Brasileiras Contemporaneas*, eds. Miriam Alves and Maria Helena Lima, 17–23. London: Mango Publishing.
Lima, V. da C. (1977) *A familia-de-santon nos Candombles Jeje-Nagos da Bahia: um estudo de relacoes intra-grupais*, Salvador, Brazil: UFBa.
———. (2000) "Ainda sobre a nacao de queto." In *Faraimara-o cacador traz alegria: mae Stella, 60 anos de iniciacao*, eds. Cleo Martins and Raul Lody, 67-80. Rio de Janeiro: Pallas.
———. (1966) "Os Obas de Xango." *Afro-Asia* 2-3, June 9–December, 5–36.
Lloyd, P.C. (1971) The Political Development of Yoruba Kingdoms in Eighteen and Nineteen Centuries Occasional Paper, no. 31. London: Royal Anthropological Institute.
Lody, R. (1998) "O rei come quiabo e a rainha come fogo. Temas da culinarian sagrada no Candomble." In *Leopardo dos Olhos de Fogo: escritos sobre a religiao dos orixas VI*, ed. C. E. M. de Moura, 145–64. Sao Paulo, Brazil: Atelie Editorial.
Lon F. (1964) *The Morality of Law*, Connecticut: Yale University Press.
Lon F. (1958) "Positivism and the Fidelity to Law-A Reply to Prof. Hart," *Harvard Law Review*, 71, 630–72.
Lovejoy, P. E. (2004) "The Yoruba Factor in the Trans-Atlantic Slave Trade." In *The Yoruba Diaspora in the Atlantic World*, eds. Toyin Falola and Matt Childs, 40–55. Bloomington: Indiana University Press.
Lucas, J.O. (1948) *The Religion of the Yorùbás*, Lagos: C.M.S.

Lum, K. A. (2000) *Praising His Name in the Dance: Spirit Possession in the Spiritual Baptist faith and Òrìṣhà Work in Trinidad, West Indies*, Amsterdam: Harwood Academic Publishers.

Marcelin, L. H. (1996) "A Invencao da Familia Afro-Americana, Familia, Parentesco e Domesticidade entre os Negros do Reconcavo da Bahia, Brasil." Ph.D. Diss, Universidade Federal do Rio de Janeiro.

Marcuzzi, M. D. (2005) "A Historical Study of the Ascendant Role of Bata Drumming in Cuban Orisa Worship." Ph.D. Diss, New York University.

Marks, M. (2001) "Introduction." In *Rhythms and Songs for the Orishas: Havana, Cuba, ca. 1957*. CD liner notes. Washington D.C.: Smithsonian Folkways Recordings.

Mason, J. (1992) *Orin Orisa: Songs for Selected Heads*, Brooklyn: Yoruba Theological Archministry.

Mason, M. A. (2002) *Living Santeria: Rituals and Experiences in an Afro-Cuban Religion*, Washington D.C.: Smithsonian Institution Press.

Matory, J. L. (2005) *Black Atlantic Religion: Tradition, Trans-nationalism and Matriarchy in the Brazilian Candomblé*, Princeton, N.J.: Princeton University Press.

———. (1994) *Sex and the Empire That is No More: Gender and the Politics of Metaphor in Oyo Yoruba Religion*, Minneapolis: University of Minnesota Press.

Maulana K. (1999) *Odu Ifa: The Ethical Teachings*, Los Angeles: University of Sankore Press.

Mc Alister, E. (2002) *Rara! Vodou, Power, and Performance in Haiti its Diaspora*, Berkeley and Los Angeles: University of California Press.

McDaniel, L. (1998) *The Big Drum Ritual of Carriacou: Praise Songs in Re-memory of Flight*, Gainesville: University Press of Florida.

McGee, A.Q (1983) "Some Mathematical Observations on the Ifa Belief System Practiced by The Yoruba People of Nigeria," *Journal of Culture and Ideas*, 1 (1), 95–114;

Mc Leod, P. (1999) (Ìyá Ṣàngó Wùmí) "World Congress Caribbean Report." *Paper Presented at the Ninth International Òrìṣà Congress, Port of Spain, Trinidad, 1999.*

Mintz, S. (1989) *Caribbean Transformations 1974*, New York: Columbia University Press.

Mischel (Henry), F. (1958) "African Power in Trinidad: The Shàngó Cult" *Anthropological Quarterly* 30: 45–59.

Morton W. P. (1964) "An Outline of the Cosmology and Cult Organization of the Ọyọ Yoruba" *Africa* 34, no 3: 243–61.

Murphy, J. M, and Mei-Mei S. eds. (2001) *Ọṣun Across the Waters: A Yorùbà goddess in Africa and the Americas*, Bloomington: Indiana University Press.

Nasiru, B. (1989) "Sàngó Ritual Pots". Unpublished M.F.A thesis, Department of Fine Arts. Ọbáfẹ́mi Awọ́lọ́wọ́ University, Ile-Ife.

Niane, D.T. (1965) *Sundiata: An Epic of Old Mali*, London: Longman Group.

Newson, L. A. (1976) *Aboriginal and Spanish Colonial Trinidad: A Study in Culture Contact*, New York: Academic Press.

Obafemi, O. (1996) *Contemporary Nigeria Theatre Cultural Heritage and Social Vision*, Bayreuth, Germany: Bayreuth African Studies Series.

Ogunbiyi, Y. (1981) Drama and Theatre in Nigeria: A Critical Source Book. *Lagos Magazine.*

Ogunbowale, P.O (1962) *Àwọn Irúnmọlẹ̀ Ilẹ Yorùbá Ibadan*, Nigeria: Evans Publisher.

Ogundeji, P. A. (1998) "The Image of Sango in Duro Ladipo's Plays." *Research in African Literatures* 29, no 2 (Summer 1998), 57–75.

———. (1988) "A Semiotic Study of Duro Ladipo Mythico-Historical Plays." Ph.D. Diss., University of Ibadan.

Ogungbile, D. (2001) "Ẹẹ̀rìndínlógún: The Seeing Eyes of Sacred Shells and Stones." In *Osun Across the Waters: A Yoruba god in Africa and the Americas*, eds. Joseph M., Murphy and Mei Mei Sanford, 89–121. Bloomington: Indiana University Press.
Ogunmola M. O. (1985) *A New Perspective to Ọyọ Empire History: 1530–1944*, Ibadan, Nigeria: Vantage Publishers.
Ojo, J.R.O. (1969) *A Short Illustrated Guide of the Museum of the Institute of African Studies*, Ile-Ife, Nigeria: University of Ife.
Okediji, M. (1989) "Òrìṣà Ikire Painting School." *Kurio Africana Journal of Art and Criticism* I, no 2, 120–31.
———. (1986) "Yoruba Paint Making Tradition." *Nigerian Magazine* 54, no 2, 19-26.
Olajubu, O.I. (1970) "*Iwi: Egúngún* Chant in Yoruba Oral Literature." M.A. thesis, University of Lagos.
Olajubu, O. (1978) "The Source of Duro Ladipo Oba Koso." *Research in African Literatures* No. 3 (Winter 1978): 327–62.
Olaoba, O. B. (2005) "Yoruba Legal Historian and Research Agenda," paper presented at the Golden Jubilee Congress of Historical Society of Nigeria, University of Ibadan, October 16–19.
Olatona, Oyegbade (Ifá and Ẹẹ̀rìndínlogún Priest). Interview conducted by the author with the Ojugbona Awo of Osogbo in Nigeria in 2001–2003.
Olatunji, O. O. (1984) *Features of Yoruba Oral Poetry*, Ibadan, Nigeria: University Press.
Olomo, A. (2003) *Core of Fire: A Path to Yoruba Spiritual Activism*, Brooklyn: Althelia Henrietta Press.
Olukoju, E. O. (1997) "Esu in the Belief of Yoruba," Orita 29 no. 1–2 (June and December).
Olunlade, Chief Ẹdẹ (1961) *A Short History*, ed. Ulli Beier, trans. I.A. Akinjogbin. Ibadan, Nigeria: G.P.S. Ministry of Education.
Olupona, J. K. (2004) "Introduction." In *Beyond Primitivism: Indigenous Religious and Modernity*, ed. Jacob K. Olupona, 1–19. New York: Routledge.
———. (1991) *Kingship, Religion and Rituals in a Nigerian Community: A Phenomenological Study of Ondo Yoruba Festivals*, Stockholm, Sweden: Almqvist and Wiksell International.
Omoniyi A. (1987) "Proverbs as Vehicles of Juristic Thought among the Yoruba" *Obafemi Awolowo University Law Journal*, January and July 1987, 1–17.
Oriki O. (1996) *The Elegant Deity of Wealth, Power and Femininity*, ed. Diedre L. Badejo, Osun Seegesi, Trenton, NJ: Africa World Press, 17.
Ortiz, F. (1995) *Cuban Counterpoint: Tobacco and Sugar*. Trans, Harriet de Onis, Durham, N.C.: Duke University Press.
———. (1984) "La Antigua Fiesta Afrocubana del Dia de Reyes." Ensayos Etnograficos (1921). Havana: Editorial de Ciencias Sociales, 41–78.
———. (1995) *"Los Instrumentos de la Musica Afrocubana*, 2 vols Havana: Letras Cubanas.
———. (1954) *Los Tambores Bata de los Yoruba Havana*, Publicigraf.
Osha, Sanya. (2016) Toyin Falola's Enchanted Yoruba Universe" *Africa Writer Magazine*, July 11.
Osha, Sanya. (2016) "In remembrance of the slave" Part 1 *The Missing Slate* February 11.
Osha, Sanya. (2016) "In remembrance of the slave" Part 11 *The Missing Slate* February 15,
Osha, Sanya. (2013) "Toyin Falola at Seventy: A Pan-Africanist Luminary for the Digital Age" In *Johannesburg Review of Books*, February 17.
Osha, Sanya. (2023) "Toyin Falola: 3 recent books that explain the work of Nigeria's famous decolonial scholar" *The Conversation*, March 23.
Oyewumi, Oyeronke. (1997) *The Invention of Woman*, Minneapolis: University of Minnesota Press.

Palmie, S. (1993) "Against Syncretism: 'Africanizing' and 'Cubanizing' Discourses in North American Orisa Worship. Counterworks, 73–103.

Pares, Luis Nicolau. (2006) *A Formacao do Candomble: Historia e Ritual da nacao Jeje na Bahia*, 1st ed. Campines, Brazil: Editora Unicamp.

———. (2004) "The Negotiation Process in Bahian Candomble." In *The Yoruba Diaspora in the Atlantic World*, eds. Totin Falola and Matt D. Child, 185–298. Bloomington: Indiana University Press.

———. (2005) "Transformation of the Sea and Thunder Voduns in the Gbe-Speaking Area and in the Bahian Jeje Candomble." In *Africa and the Americas: Interconnections during the Slave Trade*, eds. C. Curto Jose and Rene Soulodre-La France, 69–93. Trenton, N.J: Africa World Press.

Peel, John D. Y (2000) *Religious Encounter and the Making of the Yoruba*, Bloomington: Indiana University Press.

Pemberton, John, III. (2000) "Divination in Sub-Sahara Africa." In *African Art and Rituals of Divination*, ed. Alisa La Gamma, 10–21. New York: Metropolitan Museum of Art.

Peter M. (1964) "An Outline of the Cosmology and Cult Organization of the Oyo Yoruba," *Africa*, XXXIV, 3, 243–60.

Peter M., William B, and Clelland E.M. Mc (1966) "Two Studies of Divination. Introduction: The Modes of Divination, *Africa: Journal of the International African Institute* 3, no. 2, 406–31.

Picton, J. (2002) "The Horse and the Rider in Yoruba Art: Image of Conquest and Possession." *Nigeria Field* 67, no 2 (Oct 2002): III–38.

Pierson, D. (1971) *Brancos e Pretos na Bahia*, Sao Paulo, Brazil: Editora Nacional.

Prince, R. (1964) *Ifa: Yoruba Divination and Sacrifice*, Ibadan, Nigeria: Ibadan University Press.

Ramos, A. (1987) "Os mythos de Xango e sua degradacao no Brasil." In *Estudos Afro-Brasileiros: trabalhos apresentados ao ier Congresso Afro-Brasileiro reuniodos no Recific em 1934*, 49–54. Rio de Janeiro: Ariel Editora.

Ramos, M. 'Willie'. (1996) "Afro-Cuban Orisa 'Worship'." In *Santeria Aesthetics in Contemporary Latin America Art*, ed. Arturo Lindsey, 51–76. Washington D.C.: Smithsonian Institution Press.

Reis, J. J.(2003) *Rebeliao Escrava no Brasil. A historia do Levante dos Males em 1835*, Sao Paulo, Brazil: Companhia das Letras.

Reis, J. J., and Ecuardo S. (1989) *Conflito e negociacao. A Resistencia negra no Brasil escravista*, Sao Paulo, Brazil: Companhia das Letras.

Ribeiro, E. (2005) "A procura de uma borboleta preta." In *Mulheres Escrevendo: Uma Antologia Bilingue de Escritoras Afro-Brasileiras Contemporaneas*, eds. Miriam Alves and Maria Helena Lima, 26–39. London: Mango Publishing.

———. (1987) "A escritora negra e o seu ato de escrever participando." In *Criacao crioula, Nu elefante branco*, Sao Paulo: Impr. Oficial do Estado.

Rodrigues, N. (1977) *Os Africanos no Brasil*, Sao Paulo, Brazil: Companhia Editora Nacional.

Rodriguez, O. A. (1995) "Introduction." In *Sacred Rhythms of Cuban Santeria*, ed. Olavo A Rodriguez CD Liner notes. Washington D.C.: Smithsonian Folksway Recordings.

Rodriguez, V. E. (1997) "Tambores Bata." In *Instrumentos de la Musica Folclorico-Popular de Cuba*, ed. Victoria Eli Rodriguez, 2 vols, 319–43. Havana: Editorial de Ciencias Sociales.

Roland H. (1988) *The Good Things in Life: A Study of Traditional Religious Culture of the Yoruba People*, Lund, Sweden: Plus, Altra.

Saburi B. (1973) *Sources of Yoruba History*, Oxford: Oxford University Press, 1.
Samuel A. C. (1852) *A Grammar and Vocabulary of the Yoruba Language*, London: Seekley.
Samuel J. (1921) *The History of the Yorubas*, Lagos: C.M.S. Publishers.
Samuel J. (1921) *History of the Yorubas*, Westport, Connecticut: Negro Universities Press.
Sandra T. B. (1989) *Africa's Ogun: Old World and New*, Bloomington, IN: Indiana University Press, 2.
Sandra T. B. (1980). *Ogun: An Old God for a New Age*, Philadelphia: Institute for the Study of Human Issues, 47.
Sandra T. B (1980) *Ogun: An Old God for a New Age*, Philadelphia: Institute for the Study of Human Issues, 4–5.
Sansi, R. (2007) *Fetishes and Monuments: Afro-Brazilian Art and Culture in 20th Century Bahia*, New York: Berghahn Books.
Santos, Deoscoredes Maximiliano dos. (1994) *Historia de um terreiro Nago: cronica historica*, Sao Paulo, Brazil: Carthago and Forte.
Santos, Juana Elbeim dos and Deoscoredes Maximiliano Santos. (1981) "O culto dos ancestrais Bahia: o culto o eguns." In *Oloorisa: escritos sobre a religiao dos orixas*, ed. C.E.M. de Moura, 153–88. Sao Paulo, Brazil: Agora.
Santos, Maria do Rosario Carvalho. *O Caminho das Matriarcas Jeje-Nago (2001) Uma contribuicao Para a historia da religiao afro no Maranhao*, Sao Luis, Brazil: Func.
Santos, Maria Rosario Carvalho, Manoel Santos Neto. (1989) *Bomboromina: Terreiros de Sao Luis – Uma interpretacao socio cultural*, Sao Luis, Brazil: SECMA/SIOGE.
Schiltz, M. (1982) "Habitus and Peasantization in Nigeria: A Yoruba Case Study." *Man New Series* 17:728–46.
——— . (1980) "Rural-Urban Migration in Iganna." Ph.D. thesis, University of London.
Silveira, R. da. (2000) "Jeje-Nago, Yoruba-Tapa, Aon Efan, Ijexa: Processo de constituicao do candomble da Barroquinha_1764-1851." *Cultural Vozes* 6, no. 94: 80–100.
——— . (2004) *Personal communication in Luis Nicolau Pares*. May 3.
Simpson, G. E. (1980) *Religious Cults of the Caribbean: Trinidad, Jamaica, and Haiti*, Rio piedras: Institute of Caribbean Studies, University of Puerto Rico.
Smith, R.S (1969) *Kingdoms of the Yoruba*, London: Methuen.
Sobande, A. (1978) "Eewo." In *Iwe Asa Ibile Yoruba* ed. Oludare Olajubu. Ikeja: Longman Nigeria Limited.
Diagne, S. (2004) "Precolonial African Philosophy in Arabic." In *A Companion to African Philosophy*, ed. Kwasi Wiredu. Malden, MA: Blackwell Publishing Limited, 68.
Soyinka, W. (1976) *Myth, Literature and the African World*, London: Cambridge University Press.
Sublette, N. (2004) *Cuba and its Music from the First Drums to the Mambo*, Chicago: Chicago Review Press.
Tavares, I. (2000) *Xango*, Rio de Janeiro: Pallas.
Thieme, D. L.(1969) "A Descriptive Catalogue of Yoruba Musical Instruments." Ph.D. Diss., Catholic University of America.
Thompson, R. F. (1984) *Flash of the Spirit: African and Afro-American Art and Philosophy*, New York: Vintage Books.
——— . (1970) "The Sign of the Divine King: An Essay on Yoruba Beaded-Embroidered Crowns and Veil and Bird Decorations." *African Art* 113, 8–17.1.
Thornton, J. K. (1983) *The Kingdom of Kongo: Civil War and Transition, 1641-1718*, Madison: University of Wisconsin Press.
Taiwo, O. (2005). Ifa: an account of a divination system and some concluding epistemological questions. *A Companion to African Philosophy*, 304–312.

Timi de Ede, I. (1961) "Los Tambores Yoruba." *Actas del Folklore Boletin Mensual del Centro de Estudios del Folklore* I, 17–31.

Tishken, J. E. (2000) "Ethnic vs Evangelical Religions: Beyond the Teaching World Religion Approach." *History Teacher* 33, no. 3 (May 2000): 303–20.

Tobe M. C. (2003) *Finding Soul on the Path of Orisa*, Berkeley, CA: Crossing Press, 3–4.

Toyin F., (2006) "The Yoruba Nation." In *Yoruba Identity Power Politics*, eds. Toyin Falola and Genova, New York: University of Rochester Press, 30.

Trigger, B. (2003) *Understanding the Early Civilizations Cambridge*, Cambridge University Press.

Trotman, D. (1976) "The Yorùbá and Òrìṣhà Worship in Trinidad and British Guiana 1938–1970" *African Studies Review* 19, No. 2, 1–17.

Tsing, Anna. (2000) "The Global Situation." *Cultural Anthropology* 15, No. 3: 327–60.

Van D. M. (2005) "Candomble in Pink, Green and Black: Re-scripting the Afro-Brazilian Religious Heritage in the Public Sphere of Salvador, Bahia." *Social Anthropology* 13: 3–26.

Verger, P. (1999) *Notas Sobre o culto aos Orixas e Voduns na Bahia de Todos os Santos, no Brasil, e na antiga Costa dos Escravos, na África (1957)*, Sao Paulo, Brazil: Edusp.

———. (1981) *Orixas*, Salvador, Brazil: Corrupio.

Visona, M.B. (2000) "With introduction and preface by Rowland Abiodun and Suzanne Blier." In *The History of Art in Africa*, New York: Hany Abram.

Wafer, J. W. (1996) *The Taste of Blood: Spirit Possession in Brazilian Candomble*, Philadelphia: University of Alabama Press.

Warner-Lewis, M. (1996) *Trinidad Yoruba: From Mother Tongue to Memory*, Tuscaloosa: University of Alabama Press.

Welch, D. B. (2001) *Voice of Thunder, Eyes of Fire: In Search of Shango in the African Diaspora*, Pittsburgh: Dorrance Publishing.

Wescott, J. and Peter M. (1962) "The Symbolism and Ritual Context of the Yoruba Laba Shango" *Journal of the Anthropological Institute of Great Britain and Ireland* 92: 23–37.

Whitford, J. (1967) *Trading Life in Western and Central Africa, 1877*, 2nd ed London: Frank Cass.

William B. (1969) *Ifa Divination: Communication Between Gods and Men in West Africa*, Bloomington: Indiana University Press.

William, I., and Moses, O. (2008). Theories of law and morality: perspectives from contemporary African jurisprudence. *In-Spire Journal of Law, Politics and Societies*, 3(2), 151-170.

Wiredu, K. (1980) *Philosophy and an African Culture*, Cambridge: Cambridge University Press, 39.

Wood, D. (1968) *Trinidad in Transition: The Years after Slavery*, New York: Oxford University Press.

Yai, O. B. (2001) "Yoruba Religion and Globalization: Some Reflections." *Cuadernos Digitales* 15 (October 2001): 1–21.

Young, R. J.C. (1995) *Colonial Desire: Hybridity in Theory, Culture and Race*, London: Routledge.

Zuesse E.M (1979) *Ritual cosmos: The Sanctification of Life in Africa Religions*, Athens: Ohio: University Press.

Part 2

AN INTERVIEW SECTION

A CONVERSATION WITH TOYIN FALOLA

Sanya Osha: You had an extraordinary childhood by most standards. You grew up in Ibadan, a bustling metropolis but you were molded on core Yoruba values. Can you talk about what these values are, the people that guided you in learning them, and how they have shaped your life?

Toyin Falola: Answer

I'll answer your question by saying that values such as respect, diligence, accountability, truthfulness, humility, honesty, fairness, devotion and loyalty, among others, have an indestructible place in the Yorùbá world, and every member of the society is, by default, saddled with the responsibility of instilling these values into anyone, especially the younger ones. To this extent, everyone understands what is expected of all members of society in terms of moral responsibilities and would make efforts to play their part in the process. In essence, the Yorùbá people, in pre-independence Africa and the early period of post-independence Africa, did not find a shortage of avenues where they would be educated in what society expected of them. This philosophy is designed from the understanding that the people's collective identity is important and deserves to be managed by everyone so that they would not invite damnation into society or to themselves. The sociological infrastructure of the people was weaved to accommodate this sentiment in its entirety. As such, everyone understood that an elder's intervention with a child who demonstrates morally suspicious behavior is an act of social responsibility and not vilification of the child. In essence, the Yoruba society created the mental space to embrace that intervention and interjection in the spirit that it would substantially assist in structuring the society in ways that would assist the Yorùbá world to make progress.

By the time, the children who defaulted on the collective moral expectations are reprimanded by the elders, they silently but apparently adjust themselves to the moral ideology of the community to the extent that they would consciously debar themselves from committing moral offenses that would invite external intervention. This comes from two different reasons. One, a child who habitually commits moral crimes would be socially interpreted as sound evidence of failed parenting, by which case the parents, and sometimes by extension, the family unit, would have their share of the blame. Two, the child would always want to reduce, as much as possible, the attention of the public, which can lead to unwanted disciplinary measures. One would notice here that moral principles and social interactions in the Yorùbá world are intertwined. The parents come into the play owing to the understanding that as members of the social network, they are familiar with what is acceptable as a moral code and what is not. By this condition, they are expected to take critical measures to develop their children's moral standards so that they would not draw themselves into the cobweb of embarrassment, disgust, or regret. Their familiarity with society and other cultures has probably exposed them to the understanding that humans are capable of assimilating any moral ideology and compromising their values in whatever form would not be encouraged. Being a historian, I can categorically inform you that this system has helped in building the moral lifestyle of the Yorùbá people, and it was very strong in the pre-colonial time, but its potency in the aftermath of Nigeria's independence was waning considerably, especially among the elites. Since parents are an integral part of society, they understand the importance of having people around to intervene in the lives of their children as they know that they would not be everywhere with their children and would not have access to all that they are capable of doing. In essence, the saying that "oju merin nii bi'mo, igba oju nii wo (four eyes—representing two parents) give birth to a child, 200—representing the society—take charge of them)" makes appropriate meaning, as it is a body of philosophy itself that underpins the sociological process of raising children among the Yoruba people. This was how I was raised. Growing up in Ibadan during my time also meant something important, particularly in navigating adulthood and also realizing my place in the cosmos. One very crucial thing among the Yoruba people is history, and they never underestimate how events of the past can shape the activities of the present. This is logically tenable to the point that what happened in the past could be a potential reason for the eventual happenings which the physicists have given an impressive name.

According to physicists, behind every action, there is an opposite reaction to complement it. This saying has a cultural equivalence among the Yoruba people. They believe that events of the past are the foundations of actions of the present. In essence, the history of Ibadan being a solid civilization in Yorùbáland has helped its indigenes who are in alignment with its attendant greatness. Apart from being an expression of the Yorùbá sociocultural settlement where people run to for their cultural and financial transformation, Ibadan housed warriors, honorable men and women and courageous sons and daughters, whose combined efforts helped in the redefinition of the Yorùbá identity. You would not have access to the great historical exploits of the Ibadan warriors, technocrats, engineers and artists in whose names Ibadan found its astronomical bearing without aligning forces with theirs so that you would thread along their patterns. Maybe this has a connection to my trajectory in academic life. The fact that Ibadan remains the settlement, turning to the urban beauty of the contemporary time, where many first events in Nigeria took place, is an attestation to this conclusion. To a considerable extent, growing up in the city of Oluyole positively impacted my career, but that is not all.

Do you remember the catchword for the Yorùbá moral ideology? Omoluabi is a condensed expression used by the Yorùbá people to mean a number of things. In other words, core Yoruba values are summed up in that expression so that every member of the Yoruba world would find it easy to understand. Despite the variances of the Yorùbá language and culture, there is no part of the Yoruba people who do not understand the moral and ideological import of Omoluabi. They are individuals who must assimilate and then demonstrate the virtues that were mentioned earlier. Being an Omoluabi is neither gender-sensitive nor class-oriented. Members of the elite class would be evaluated based on their behavioral consistency in relation to the ideology of Omoluabi. This means that anyone who occupies any position in the Yorùbá world is analyzed based on their ability to comport themselves and act in accordance with the Yorùbá ideological and moral convictions expressed in that word. This is important to the extent that people who violate the basic principles of being an Omoluabi would be invited to a public admonition and not spared a lot of criticism by necessary authorities. There was a cultural check and balance. Meanwhile, those who are at the lower rung of power in the society too are not looked down on and would be reprimanded too on the occasion that they violate the principles of Omoluabi. As long as the individual desires to be a good representative of the family, they will always maintain this code.

Underneath these ideas are values such as respect. The Yorùbá people place a premium on respect for others and for constituted authorities. Contrary to a misconception that Yorùbá people place a strong emphasis on respect, even for elders who are on the wrong side of moral principles, Yorùbá people actually do the opposite. They are concerned primarily about human dignity and integrity and would not encourage taking advantage of others, perhaps over the assumption that they have weak moral standards. Respect for others even when they are wrong would create the atmosphere for a fair hearing where supposedly right ones would have a better opportunity to see things from different and uncommon perspectives. Without respect for others, this right would be automatically violated. Meanwhile, their concern about respect is not monodirectional. They recognize the place of respect too for the younger ones, but this, itself, is a body of philosophical understanding that would deserve a different place for exploration. As much as they identify respect, the Yorùbá people understand the place of diligence too in their moral and ideological solidarity. Many dictionaries define diligence as conscientiousness or determination or perseverance when pursuing a goal. It is undebatable that I am determined when I place my attention on an important goal. I don't falter; I don't renege. I get what I want as much as I desire them.

I cannot tell you that I satisfy all the moral codes required by the Yorùbá world to be called an Omoluabi, but I can confidently tell you that I maintain a high standard in every one of the codes. For example, the Yoruba world understands that the foundation of being an Omoluabi is to be accountable, which is not in the area of taking records for yourself personally, but being, firstly, responsible for the upbringing of others for the enhancement of a strong society that would be safe for all. Apart from the extension of this accountability trait to my work ethics, I have been accountable to a number of the younger people in my life, and that is a satisfaction of the code of accountability as conceived by the Yorùbá people. The beauty of this philosophical mindset is that it is not race-sensitive, and neither is it identity-restricted. To this extent, I have been an instrument to many people's career trajectories while simultaneously making life easier for the ones I work with. The most amazing part of this is that it has become an integral part of my thought process, so much so that I do that unconsciously. I would not have advanced this much without showing the value of accountability that I was taught as a child. There is not so much difference between being accountable and being truthful. Truthfulness is the next Yorùbá value up in line for discussion; it is a subset of the former. One has to be incurably truthful among the Yoruba people.

As already implied, humility remains one of the most important aspects of the Yoruba moral worldview. One needs to be humble, not because humility is necessary to win people's admiration but because humility opens up people to others to make them see through their vulnerabilities. People who are humble are always given access to other people's private experiences under the understanding that they would not misjudge or misunderstand them. Apart from this, the Yorùbá culture emphasizes humility in people so that they would create an atmosphere for heart-to-heart conversations with others, as people naturally have the tendency to limit their engagement with others that are perceived as lacking humility. Knowledge is acquired by individuals who have humble spirits. The ones who possess knowledge would not hand it out to those whom they see as boastful. In essence, humility is a defining attribute that the Yorùbá people place so much premium on. Meanwhile, they are also concerned about honesty and fairness. Honesty is that virtue that one cannot shortchange for whatever reason. Being honest is important, and it is a good character trait. Honest people are plain and have no reason for deception. The Yorùbá people, irrespective of location, are also concerned about fairness to others. To be fair to others means that one has a place for their differences in one's heart. One understands that circumstances sometimes are responsible for the formulation of human behavior, and until one walks into another man's shoes, it would be difficult to understand why they make the choices that they make. In essence, what is required is to be fair to people irrespective of who and where they are from. All these have governed my behavior with people and organizations from the beginning of time. You cannot understate the critical importance of honesty in securing the trust of others. This is connected to devotions. One has to be generally devoted to one's goals and aspirations to become very successful in life. The saying that "a rolling stone gathers no moss" readily comes to mind here. If I had not been devoted to my calling, it would probably have been difficult for me to attain success.

Sanya Osha: In *Counting the Tiger's Teeth,* the Yorùbá deities are foregrounded and duly honored. You also analyze the much-ignored Agbekoya rebellion. Do you mind discussing the influence of Yoruba cultural background in instigating and executing the war? How did the war shape you personally and what did you learn about broader Yoruba culture and its place within the larger Nigerian configuration?

Toyin Falola: Answer

In many societies, pre-modern and modern, war was an integral part of the civilizational evolution of the people. Although conceived as hostile engagements and interactions between groups, wars come with the opportunity to improve one's knowledge about technology. I have mentioned it elsewhere that warring was central to survival in the past, given the aggressive desires of groups and civilizations to conquer others. For weak groups to survive, they needed to develop better skills and knowledge that would propel them to make inventions with which they could face their adversaries. In pre-colonial times, these people were assured that the potential war-mongering civilizations were doing so to expand their economic and political landscapes. Beyond it, however, the orientation of engineering controversy as the force of democratic change was accommodated by the people of the period. The respect and dignity of labor that the people enjoyed was cast on the knowledge that everyone must respect others irrespective of social class. By satisfying these basic principles of existence, there would be protracted peace and stability to bring about economic success and transformation of people in that environment. Although external contradictions happened from time to time, they had measures by which they responded to volatile issues that could instigate chaos or prompt disorder. The history of the Yoruba people is unpretentious to its association with deities, as these are considered cosmic figures that are represented in physical forms for their time spent as humans. The realization of the deities happens in two different categories: one, in the physical category and two, in the metaphysical world. Those who came as humans exhibited extraordinary traits that showcased them as superhumans. Their preternatural qualities assisted them in navigating their ways and contributing essentially to the Yorùbá civilization during their existence. These deities have different qualities. There are some that are concerned about human capacity and ability to coordinate activities of the people. These ones emphasize leadership traits and are continually interested in the protection of the people. Irrespective of the circumstances, they are always interested in the coordination of the people. Across the Yorùbá world, people adopt these deities, adapting their characteristics as the basis of their own lifestyle. It is, therefore, understandable that each family and clan from the Yorùbá world has their separate deities that they identify with and whose philosophical leanings they embrace. There are deities that are for fertility, transformation and opulence, while there are the ones that guide people against aggressions of whatever sort. The embrace of their identity has contributed to their sustenance as a race in every place they are found. But beyond the politics of deities as cosmic forces, there is the realization of these beings as guardians of virtues and principles. Their traits help people to decide on their lifestyles.

The extent that the people and the deities share a mutual interest in the community of the Yorùbá people is what necessitates invoking deities whenever they are in need of the actions of any of them. For instance, deities in charge of fertility are summoned to intervene in the marital affairs of couples who are yet to bear children. When faced with imminent violence and aggression from expansionists, the deities in charge of protection are invoked to guide the people and enhance their safety in whatever embroilment they find themselves. In the occasion of many of my books on the nineteenth century and specifically the one you referenced in your question, the book entitled *Counting the Tiger's Teeth*, I chronicled the history of the Yoruba people vis-a-vis the imperial imposition of the expansionists who have dominated the political and, by extension, the economic space of the African people. The cultural beauty of the group is expressed in a communal identity that they mutually accept as their cross. Even when there are events that trigger internal contradictions and ravaging controversy, when it is an issue that threatens their collective or communal safety, they always combine forces to resist external actions that undermine their existence. They did this in the case of the Yoruba-Fulani aggression of 1840, where the Yorùbá people made Ibadan their outpost, where military intelligence was coordinated, personnel trained, and their strategies organized. Typical of the warlords of Ibadan, they displaced their enemies and forced them into submission.

To understand how the Yoruba cultural background influenced the Agbekoya uprising in the mid-twentieth century, one needs to understudy the values of the Yorùbá people. I have mentioned some of them.

The colonial government of the period had become unquestionable, pushing the people to erect a superior posture, not only in their character of totalitarian governance but also in their unyielding nature in democratic engagement. That necessitated the introduction of all manners of policies, including the ones that threatened the security of the people in every sense of the word. When economic security was taken from the people, political security and social security became a dispensable victim in the process. The farmers who were the economic oxygen of the government were severely exploited with the introduction of heartrending tax policies that watered down their efforts. The government was evidently insensitive to the complex intricacies that surrounded farming, especially at a time of less technology for the enhancement of the farmers. Having undergone a series of challenges from seeking access to land for cultivation, the colonial government became controlling and wanted to determine how and when farmers enjoyed their hard-earned labor. Although the Yorùbá people appeared to be cornered by the superior military might of Europe, if it got to risking their lives to save their dignity, nothing stopped them.

The place of cultural identity was espoused in the collective actions against the emerging unpopular government policies that wrecked their economic system. Having the economic power, the Yorùbá people of the period knew that it was tantamount to having military capacity. The only difference, they believed, was that one involved a pure adoption of violence while the other embraced tactics. Decapitating the economic power of the colonial system was considered very instrumental in their liberation agenda. Meanwhile, the Yorùbá people of the West African region were one of the most consistent producers of cocoa in the continent, which meant that the heart of the colonial economy in Africa was metaphorically controlled by them. What they did with that power was to invoke their cultural understanding of communal togetherness, which, for one, prompted them to create a group that would represent the interests of the farmers. When the government appeared hellbent on increasing their tax, and it seemed that it would be successful as the indigenous government was in connivance, they organized themselves into formidable groups that spoke to power and voiced their opinions about issues that affected them. Farmers would ensure that the new marketing system did not consume them through the manipulative efforts of the colonial powers.

To ask about how that experience, which I witnessed as a child, shaped me personally is to nudge me to begin to unpack the layers of transformational values that I derived from that single encounter. While this space and time would not allow me to have full exploration of it, doing a little bit of the work would actually suffice. I was educated, first, about the power of collectivism, especially in relation to its critical place in getting people their deserved status, respect, dignity and honor. To understand how deeply the Yorùbá people value communal life and collective ideology, one would have to get familiar with some of their philosophical sayings. The Yorùbá people have the saying that "Adede owo kan, ko gbe'ru d'ori" (one does not lift loads to the head with one hand), "Agbajo owo la fi n soya" (there is pride in a single voice), among others that highlight within their epistemic making the essence and importance of togetherness and speaking in one voice. As a child who identifies with such a cultural space, one will first understand that there is a fiercer force when people organize themselves as a unit. One will marvel at how formidable they could be by merely constituting themselves as a group and committing their energy to their common course. From my formative experience, I began to understand the very importance of power concentrated in the people, and that has continued to guide me to date.

As funny as it would sound, I also understood, from the war, that life is made up of forces and energies and that as humans, who themselves are constitutive of these forces, they would have to negotiate a number of things to become free or have access to liberation. The colonial imperialists formed great forces against the indigenous African people. In this case, they formed a force against the Yorùbá community by standing firmly in the way of the farmers and remaining intransigent and unperturbed by their worries. Meanwhile, these Yoruba people had talents, they were dedicated, and they worked very hard. They wanted to have success as evidence of their hard work. But nature itself is complex. One would face numerous challenges in the process of making a name and achieving one's ambitions in life. It would, therefore, become very clear that while talent may offer one the resources with which one can combine and produce results, one needs a measure of toughness to weather the storms that would come eventually. If the farmers had refused to organize themselves into a formidable unit to challenge the excessive power abuse demonstrated by the colonial power and, in the stead, accepted the unruly administrative atrocities committed against them, they would have created a wrong impression that would warrant similar maltreatment in their future engagements. In essence, it prepared me to be ready to face challenges.

Although there are some political sides to the story, as the nascent political leader, Chief Obafemi Awolowo, of the region was excommunicated in the period when the taxes were introduced, his return, however, brought different dynamics to the controversy. Standing in for the farmers where it mattered, the issue became a political problem that demanded immediate attention from the government. He negotiated with them by being their mouthpiece to the colonial government, and eventually, the issue became quenched by his intervention. Whereas others have equal rights to be recognized for their outstanding actions and contributions toward bringing the issue under control, the fact that the Yorùbá regional power was potent cannot be overemphasized. The people realized that the Yorùbá people have human and natural resources which they could use to their advantage if an occasion called for it. They earned their respect as people who stood up for themselves even when it appeared that the government was unyielding and strongly adamant. I believe that the war sent a very powerful message to the Western powers about the ability of people to coordinate themselves when faced with an imminent threat that could affect them negatively. Even if they did not have Western education, they, however, had the power to organize themselves and ask the right questions about their existence. Nigeria owes it to accord the Yorùbá people respect.

It was at a moment when a predatory government was seeking to increase the economic woes of their victims with backbreaking laws and levies was done around indigenous metaphysics. The people apparently stood no chance against their colonizers because it was characteristic of the West to employ the state power to defend whatever policy they introduced to their subject. In this case, the Agbekoya group was inviting government wrath for daring to challenge and question their authority. Their commitment to the course of freedom from these imposed laws and unjustified fees was underscored by the understanding that they would either confront the longstanding anomaly of tax imposition or continue to have occasional experiences of maltreatment and misgovernance. Although the British had the security agencies at their disposal, the Agbekoya group would not cede their economic profits to the West, even if it meant undergoing brutal reprisals at the hands of these postcolonial characters. They persisted and deployed all the available means within their control to challenge the hegemonic structure so that they would reverse the tax policy introduced. In the same way, they wanted to reduce the unbridled braggadocio of the government, which has undermined their efforts for a long time.

As a younger person, I experienced at close quarters the deployment of Oogun (charms or juju), which these Yorùbá agitators employed to challenge all the government's forces against freedom. Of course, one would have heard times without numbers that African charms were nonexistent or ineffective compared to how it has always been discussed. However, one who had the experience would not rush to make such a comment because what they have seen would always negate cooked narratives that merely want to discredit their capacity by distorting the information. What reinstated the confidence of these people was the knowledge that they had something with which they would confront the British government. The fact that the British were not also interested in indulging what they considered the excesses of the farmers meant that they were committed to going head-to-head with them. This made the situation more explosive and intensified the way their warring engagement was to be unleashed. Aware that these farmers would not be intimidated, they deployed more security operatives to combat them and scare them to their pants. But this tactic was not enough to dampen the Agbekoya group's spirit.

Truth to the potency of their charms, they continued to challenge their putative opponents, the British, with a level of resistance that defied the latter's planned aggression. The farmers trooped out, and in a very short time, they became a formidable force, matching the government forces, power to power and tactics to tactics. They demonstrated some level of confidence as they continued without stopping their desire to fight for their freedom from all manners of interest groups.

Here, I understood immediately that until individuals decide to confront their challenges, they will not cease to experience layers of threats and vulnerabilities that can potentially consume them. They demonstrated effectively that until you decide to stand tall against obstacles, you would not have the opportunity to achieve a level of success that would be sustainable. The British government realized then that there would be more resistance from the people if they came up with predatory ideas that exposed them to dangers of all kinds.

Meanwhile, they met their equals in that period. The security operatives deployed to bring down the farmers and erase their economic values were given appropriate warring displays that made them rethink their aggression against the people. This helped in many ways, but it earned them the respect they deserved. The experience immensely shaped me because it taught me, among other things, the connections between metaphysical powers and supernatural existence. These two are keenly associated with the patterns that the cosmic community works with. In addition to this, it taught me that Yorùbá people are tolerant but not stupid. On the first point, there is general knowledge that supernatural forces in the universe are alive. That is the reason that influenced the creation of religious identity by people in the end, as they understand that these cosmological forces are capable of being domesticated. They are therefore convinced that it is through their domestication that they can invoke them for concrete results.

On the second point, Yorùbá has always shown their tendency to take people into their circle. They have an understanding that everyone wants to be happy, regardless of what their cultural or religious views are, and instead of viewing them from a negative perspective even when they have not lived with them, they would offer such people the opportunity to coexist with them in a bid to expand their social networks. But this does not mean that they are stupid regardless. They were opening their hearts and arms to people who might have been misunderstood and exploited in the past. But it seemed apparent that they would not allow anyone to ridicule them.

This orientation, for example, compelled them to stand against the British government for daring to impose taxes that would take away their financial opportunities. Although the Agbekoya experience happened in the last century, their resistance culture to anything that threatened their safety predates this particular timeline. There have been a series of internal and external exploitative advancements that were resisted in similar versions. This indicates the power of human thinking, the knowledge to know when to challenge others and stand against them when their rights are trampled upon, the collective willpower to resist every instance of imposition and dictation, and the tenacity to continue regardless of their awful experiences. Although wars are brutal, then that of the Agbekoya left an important impression and imprint in the hearts of people like me. It made me appreciate the power inherent in united groups. Farmers came out to challenge the established hegemony, which was an important lesson about building a formidable network. The efforts would have been easily sabotaged, especially by the sellouts who would want to explore the opportunities inherent in it to get to the side of the oppressors.

In the same way, the war educated me about endurance. While the British government had the power to deploy more security operatives to fight on their behalf, the indigenous Agbekoya group, too, was very stubborn about their agitations. Although they banked on their charms and the metaphysical power to face the government's police, they lacked the military tactics to guarantee their safety, protection, and continued existence. It is almost impossible for groups to successfully face a government and win because governments always have the power to deploy state resources to achieve their desires while the group has limited access to all these important things. However, despite the obvious reduction of their human power, the Agbeko endured. They remained steadfast and uncompromising in their quest for policy reconsideration. Therefore, it was evident that without the government shifting its ground, the group would continue and ensure that their endurance remained till the last minute. Of course, this tactic worked, and it has also proved in a life situation that endurance is a recipe for success. In all my personal involvement or life's pursuits, I have always demonstrated endurance, which explains why I continue to get results even where I have least imagined them. They succeeded against the British government because what they wanted and agitated for was eventually considered.

Sanya Osha: Can you discuss your days at the then University of Ife (now Obafemi Awolowo University (OAU) and the great minds in the humanities and social sciences that influenced the zeitgeist during your time there? In other words, to what extent would you say your involvement at Ife defined your intellectual trajectory?

Toyin Falola: Answer

People all across the world are shaped by the ideas of their environment, and by the environment, there is the temptation to include one's age, physical landscape, era and ideological tenor within one's timeline. If we conceive the environment this way, we have the liberty to look at the University of Ife (now Obafemi Awolowo University) within these variances of its realization, starting with age. The university was established when agitations for knowledge-producing centers in the colonial landscape in Africa reached the rooftop. Western education was apparently a popular bride, and it was more than necessary to have one. Apart from the values associated with having a university education during the said period, the country's future was calculatedly structured around anyone who had successful academic exposure. Meanwhile, the dream of making an impact in independent Nigeria was worthwhile, especially for anyone who understood the value of being instrumental in revolutionary engagements. OAU became very clear about its mission; it was an institution that was concerned about actual and thorough intellectual engagement to be garnished with cultural traditions. People wanted to draw from such a budding academic environment and contribute to its growth in whatever capacity they could.

With regards to its physical landscape, there is no coincidence that the school, whose motto is "For Learning and Culture," is located in Ile-Ife, where the Yorùbá people collectively agree is their source of existence. Apart from being an inexhaustible source of cultural traditions with its limitless ideas and values, Ife served as the shield to people and figures who wanted to take some adventure into the fabric of their Yorùbá identity. In essence, the environment became an accessory to the accumulation of knowledge for students, and it was understandable why it became the choice of many scholars to teach and conduct their research. The centrality of Ile-Ife to the Yorùbá culture and civilization affords people there, including academics and researchers, to have access to people, individuals and personalities that have numerous ideas to offer them and transform their existence. In terms of the necessary human personnel needed to actualize the dream, there are innumerable scholarly resources that are available in the place for consultation and mentorship about the Yorùbá epistemology and ontology, among others. As much as the geographical landscape offered this opportunity, it also was a forceful influence on what we call Nigeria's education system from its time, even to the contemporary period.

With regard to the era, the time I was a student at OAU was filled with individuals who had a matchless and immeasurable zeal and wanted to be of value to Nigeria's dream. It was a time when parents participated in the inculcation of values into the students as a routine and their own contributions to the development of the country. Parents were genuinely interested in the progress of their children to the extent that they participated actively in driving knowledge to them. While the university was a place where you acquire theoretical ideas and knowledge, the house was where you learned about ethics, values, and moral principles, unlike the contemporary time when all these items of knowledge are left to the teachers alone. Of course, it is because the parents are "busy." Undergraduates, therefore, were not in a race to acquire all the wealth of the world even when they were still under the tutelage of teachers; they were not concerned about how they would survive in their postgraduate experience as adults, as there were necessary government and non-government agencies that were ready incorporate them into the labor market, apparently because they were well educated and well-behaved. Today, fortunes are spent on a child's education and, by extension, their good behavior.

Regarding the ideological tenor of our time, education was seen as power, and with power, it was almost certain that one would have access to closed doors. And there was no better means of bragging than a career in Western education then. Going to school automatically earned one the respect of peers and the recognition of the community. You were most likely going to be seen as honorable and be well respected for that, given the understanding that an educated individual always showed signs of intellectual greatness. They were different, outstanding and unique in everything in which they did or were involved. It is not coincidental, therefore, that people's moral and ideological values grew in accordance with their academic accomplishments during the time. Apart from the decision to become the best to improve the conditions of one's background (family), the time of our university education was when ideology was strictly important to people. Graduates did not, in any way, compromise the standards of society to satisfy their provincial intentions and would not be an accessory to the deliberate ruination of the moral fabric of society. We wanted to become active members to turn things around in the country, and OAU was ready to assist us to achieve our collective ambitions.

Having defined what I conceive as an environment in the above paragraphs, one would not be caught surprised that the period was laced with people of strong intellectual and moral values. I remember a colleague

(Ogunkanmi) with whom we undertook academic lectures and activities together. His commitment to knowledge-related engagement and the zeal to become better in what he did were enough inspiration for me. Do you know that people who are ready to learn or who are open to knowledge always have sharp minds in decoding messages, even in unconventional sources? Consider, for example, that humans are capable of learning from other humans when they calm their nerves. I learn from individuals more than I learn in classrooms. I read people more than I read books. And these qualities have continued to contribute to my success, especially in the academic community. Relating to the individual I mentioned above, one would understand that life's ambitions are worth taking when one does not want to plunge into the abyss of error. You cannot but increase your reading when you have these types of individuals around you. They would motivate you, not by telling you to come to a library to read, but by their unwavering dedication to their own academic engagement.

The OAU of our period was one with impressive faculty power, and as a result, there was a transfer of knowledge to the students easily and effectively. Many of the teachers automatically took the role of mentors and counselors, as they brought us in to educate us on issues that were beyond the academic environment. Quite a number of us understood the magnitude of "outside-school responsibility," and to rise to these challenges or necessities, we were educated to first handle our education appropriately so that we would have the resources with which we would seal with external realities. Although there were signs of globalization in that period, we did not actually experience it in the raw form that it is today. Nonetheless, we got the necessary values that were important enough to help us navigate human existence beyond our time as students. Since the time was only a fledging moment in African intellectual rediscovery where the items of history were limited to the ones introduced by the Europeans, we became very active in changing the status quo so that we would offer a new direction to African history and also pioneer theories to understand them. Our teachers were influential in this. They assisted us significantly and transformed our academic skills and values.

Obafemi Awolowo University represents an African knowledge institution that prioritizes education in its entirety and gives its leaning toward African epistemological terrain with its knowledge system. It helped in molding my views about life generally, and I will tell you how. In the Yorùbá worldview, knowledge has an indestructible order, and elders who, in the care of my experience at OAU, are scholars would take conscious responsibility to ensure that every person learned. This was possible because they were generally seen as the repository, given the vast array of experiences that they had and the practical situations they had dealt with. As they were assisting us in getting into the core areas of academic excellence, there were a few of them that made extra effort to ensure that we transformed our raw talent into results. That I experienced academic tutelage with the man I mentioned earlier is all you need to understand about the critical point of OAU to knowledge production in Africa. There seems to be a truth in the saying that a golden fish has no hiding place. This individual demonstrated to us early that the more an individual dedicated their time to what they valued, the more values they would add to themselves. While we were struggling to grab the understanding that undergraduate education was brief but everlasting, he had already made an impressive landmark for himself. Perhaps, the aura of the OAU environment or the allure of the infrastructure there was the motivation for academic engagement that we had. It cannot be overemphasized that the education that we acquired was solidified by these factors. Although there were times dedicated to fun even as undergraduate students, we, however, did not compromise academic excellence on the altar of self-aggrandizement that would bring us untold mental or intellectual damage. We persevered and became relentless, and the signal that we were serious helped influence the decisions of our academic leaders to direct us where it was needed. Scholars from different places outside Nigeria related to us accordingly, and we had no problem with our self-esteem as undergraduate students. We were meant to understand that the limits to our growth were the ones we planted there and that, by nature, humans are not innately restricted on how far they can go in life. We inculcated this idea very quickly enough, and we became stronger in pursuing our dreams. We were active both academically and politically. The scholars we had then were not the docile type who was restricted by forces against their will.

I was a very active student as an undergraduate in OAU. In fact, my culture of dedication and seriousness to issues was foregrounded there. I cultivated that idea as a student while in school. There are many other people who we went to school together in OAU who are doing exceptionally fine in their engagements. The beautiful thing is that the influence that these sets of people had on us was not limited by the different career paths. There were students who we looked up to even in different departments because of the understanding that they were doing exceptionally well in their engagements as students. All these were things that ignited the zeal in me, and to say I am indebted to the people I attended school with is to mention, in passing, how their involvement in my life has yielded profoundly beautiful results. My view about life, the philosophy I carved from it, the understanding of the complexity of human nature and the fact of social togetherness are things that I learned from the school and have continued to stay with me in my current journey. From teachers to friends, colleagues to teammates, libraries to research or reading centers within the university, I am highly indebted to the foundational structure erected in me and everyone who attended OAU at that time. Ife has always been great and no one needs to tell it to the world any longer. It is already doing the job itself.

Beyond the instrumentality of teachers and colleagues in creating an important attitude to education, the period in question was a time when there was a rise in radicalism. It seemed that the commitment of the Nigerian nationalists who confronted the British government with their intellectual power when seeking independence did not go into extinction with the emergence of the country as an independent country. From all indications, it hibernated and became available for use anytime people considered it important. The unfolding events of the post-independence period revealed that totalitarian regimes and undemocratic leadership had not gone with the colonizers as the new Nigerian leaders became very disposed to the British government style. Meanwhile, at the pinnacle of British misrule, the people of the country stood to resist pervasive misgovernance and heartrending administrative behaviors that characterized the time, and now that the new Nigerian leaders are exhibiting similar attitudes while in power, the people stood to them with a redefined culture of resistance to reclaim their rights and set them well in the right direction. More than two decades after Nigeria's independence, people have not experienced the dividends of democracy and were instead exposed to all manners of leadership diabolism. In essence, the people promoted radicalism as a national attitude against the government by getting involved in engagements that called out the leaders and powerful forces impeding their growth in all ramifications. From the people in the intellectual domain to the common ones, their agitation was united, which was demonstrated in different ways. The radicalism of the period was well handled, better organized, and carefully planned with a topnotch execution strategy employed to reduce the overbearing influence of the political class. This was recreated within the academic community in many Nigerian schools, and students like us began to understand the centrality of the led to every form of governance. The radical movement educated us appropriately that people are at the center of every government and would therefore not be tossed around when they are disrespected, or their fundamental rights are taken away. We took part in the struggle and supported movements against issues considered threats to the community or us. Whereas as we participated in such engagement, we were assimilating the knowledge that sometimes radical movements are all it needs to challenge a government that is unyielding and unresponsive to people.

I should remind you, too, that this was a political period in Nigeria's and Africa's history when military regimes were almost the norm rather than the exemption to the administrative system. I, however, do not need to remind you that military government was a catalyst for sociocultural and sociopolitical repulsion. Apart from their insensitivity to human freedom, their crystal-clear desire for the destruction of human dignity was a thing that deserved the repudiation of any people who were still interested in their dignity. The military rank and file and the democrat government representatives imposed the military on the Nigerian populace. The former was actively involved apparently because they believed it was the responsibility of the military men to intervene whenever it appeared that people were being mal-governed. On the side of the collaboration of the democratically elected leaders, however, their deliberate acts of fund mismanagement, abuses of public offices, and their eternal desires for personal aggrandize were too much an indulgence that reasonable people could tolerate. This brought the innocent ones into an avoidable dilemma. The military was not desirable as a suitable replacement for government officials abusing the office, while the democratic leaders were deep-seated in their corrupt indulgences and that in itself would potentially wreck the future of the innocent generation to come.

Even when we knew the overbearing tendency of the military regimes, we joined anti-military agitations and organized demonstrations that would signal the dictators at the helm of affairs of general discontentment against their totalitarian ideals. I need to reiterate that going against the military and their activities pointedly like this meant that you are ready to bear the consequences of your actions when you are on their radar for revenge.

It means you have chosen lack of freedom over the freedom you enjoy. It means you have particularly exposed the people around you to avoidable challenges. It was so common that they used guerilla tactics to capture their critics and subject them to excessive punitive actions. We continued, and as a budding academic, I learned important lessons from all of these engagements. I continued without stopping and would always conclude that the emergence of colonizers in Africa brought more problems for the people than it brought development. The awareness underscored this conclusion that military actions were not in existence before the ascension of the Europeans to African space. This, therefore, question the importance of democracy as it appears then those undemocratic cultures exhibited by the military were necessary to arrive at democracy. Whatever it was, people resisted it.

Given all the conditions the people are in, scholars understood that scholars concentrated on finding diplomatic solutions to the administrative problems ravaging the country. Although they were not the ones to enforce the government system to be operated with the political class, it is nonetheless part of their professional assignment to seek alternative means of governance so that it would be beneficial to all. Meanwhile, the period was filled with the belief that socialism was good as it reflected the people's sociocultural interpretation of life. They understood, for example, that things should be of value and advantage to the people irrespective of their status within the society and on the occasion that they are not even benefiting maximally from a government, they should not be persecuted or exposed to unbearable social circumstances. They calculated, for instance, that such conditions would always be used to create chaos by which condition the society would be ridden by chaotic struggles that make sink the moral and ideological fabrics of the society. Experts, therefore, began to seek a great alternative to their country's declining economic and political values. Such has always been the way of the intellectuals as they are always seeking to be instrumental in the growth and development of society.

It was a period characterized by different uncoordinated events that were responded based on the circumstances of postcolonial Nigerian politics. Of course, doing all these things meant that we were paying dearly for our resistance, and this, again, is what motivated another line of philosophy in my career. It was then when I knew that as much as you desire great things in life, there must be the willpower to undergo the critical challenges in actualizing that ambition. While the military was busy waging ideological wars and hostilities against us, the people continued and refused to be consumed by the negativity of the time. It persisted, but people too resisted as that will not only determine their survival as social beings, but it would also dictate how they would be governed eventually. I feel some sense of nostalgia when I remember events of the period because each of these actions then brought everyone closer to the understanding that even when life throws challenges at individuals, once they have a clear picture of what they want and where they are going in mind, it would always be a success story for them in the long run. That was what energized us. The spirit of togetherness helped reveal the ideological fertility of the time, which brought to the open the alternative political ideas that were ushered into existence.

Sanya Osha: You were trained as a historian but increasingly your work has become both interdisciplinary and transdisciplinary in scope and nature. Can you describe the background and reasons behind this shift?

Toyin Falola: Answer

If we look at education beyond the prism of Western epistemologies, we will notice that education is not meant to be restricted to a particular discipline. In fact, when we probe Western education in a deeper way, we would notice that it is not consistent with the superficial division that separates one discipline from another. Consider, for example, individuals who have gone to study the English language at the university, they would invariably study the English culture manifested in different forms. Some would inculcate the dressing culture of the English people, while others would have to learn about their social values. Meanwhile, when one gets to this level of academic relationship with English, the probability is that one is already walking the line of their history. In essence, their knowledge of English history constitutes another line of academic engagement that they have inadvertently acquired. While these things can be described as superficial interrogation of disciplines and professions, it, nonetheless, proves that rigid professional delineation is practically impossible. This would, therefore, show that there is no absolute consistency in the establishment of discipline in accordance with career creation and pursuance. All these nuances are what make the educational system appear how it does.

In the African epistemological terrain, however, strict division of disciplines is nearly nonexistent in many of the cultural traditions of the continent. People acquire knowledge from various fields with the understanding that it would be valuable in one way or the other as they navigate their existence in life. Quite a number of African people, especially the Yoruba people, have been programmed this way, and it seems they are making it a cultural idea that evolved through the consistency in that behavior. You would notice that even in contemporary times after graduates are done with their academic engagements in school, they are recruited into apprenticeship education so that they would understand ideas that govern other career paths, make good decisions for themselves and to also navigate their world properly. Although some have expressed their concerns about this development, I consider it as a reenactment of what has become a crucial part of the Yorùbá world and their epistemic perception.

In the pre-colonial Yoruba world, learners who are enrolled in fashion designing are informally recruited as market experts in the evening because their parents indulged them to oversee their subsistence marketing, and that again became an avenue to learn and elaborate their knowledge. In essence, my interdisciplinary and transdisciplinary considerations are an extension of what happens to be a cultural program in me.

That said, my training as a historian is the only academic experience that offers the most flexible opportunities for multidisciplinary education and transdisciplinary possibility. Remember that History is the grand master of every other discipline.

In every career path, what people do is to learn history. I expatiate the argument by saying that when we understudy an equation or formula used in Mathematics, we are only merely downloading historical efforts put in place by another individual. In essence, when we read the accumulated engagement of the individual that propounded it, there is every likelihood that we would come across the aspect when they invented the formula. In other words, we are learning history in that sense. When you go to a doctor to complain about back pain or report a tumor that you feel is in your head, the doctor poses some random questions to you. Your response would be matched with what he had experienced in the past. If it correlates, he will describe how you feel, which would automatically be in sync with what previous patients felt in a similar circumstance. He would prescribe drugs to you based on similar experiences he had in the past. In essence, doctors too are historians. If these professions are duplications of history, how much more is History as a profession itself?

I draw inspiration from a number of things, the chief of which is the Yoruba's knowledge epistemologies. As I have already implied, the Yoruba's perception of knowledge is one that recognizes having useful information in several fields so that one can have diverse intellectual resources with which one can see the world and respond to its varying challenges. Challenges, in this sense, do not mean negative experiences. Anything capable of triggering a response from people is considered one. Understanding that Africa's cultural history is one that is laden with numerous events and activities that stretch across different professional disciplines. A person cannot remain frozen in the intellectual domain by refusing to explore the various aspects that are explorable from it. Of course, we acquire knowledge from the teachers in school, but our parents, the primary agents of socialization, and society continue to educate us about the vast aspects of learning that we are yet to understand. When we have access to these things, it behooves us to replicate them in our academic undertakings, and coincidentally, they are not things that can be fixed exclusively in the wings of History alone as a profession.

I have written works on Yorùbá metaphysics and I have done impressive studies on the literature of the people at the same time. You cannot underplay the contagious spark of multidisciplinary possibility that is inherent in people's epistemology. Meanwhile, the metaphysics of the Yorùbá people, while it could have been taught as history in the university, remains an independent aspect of learning that matches its global contemporaries, such as the metaphysics of Greek philosophers and the ones of Latin origin. However, all these would not achieve their maximum potential if they were still locked eternally within the confines of History as a discipline. In fact, the understanding that Western education is expanding in its influence and efficiency is associated with the spread of these knowledge systems they began with is enough motivation that expanding the historical system and ideas of the African people can have an enormous impact on their knowledge production and in the process, their civilization. They have been able to separate from various knowledge epistemologies that are not used to fortify their education and also their civilization. In essence, scholars from Africa must, as a matter of necessity and expediency, sieve the knowledge that they acquired away from the prism of professional disciplines so that they would discover the areas where they have the capacity to function to the fullest.

While I have been acknowledged as a historian of note in the continent, I cannot undermine the effectiveness of my intellectualism in other disciplines because the more I look into the content of knowledge that I have acquired as a historian, the more I uncover vast areas of knowledge that can be useful for the enhancement and restoration of Africa's dignity. While the writings I did on Yorùbá metaphysics opened my eyes to the myriad of African intellectual resources, especially in understanding seemingly puzzling phenomenon, I cannot emphasize enough how many other areas are there to be explored in the Yorùbá world. To that extent, we would be doing a disruptive educational engagement that would challenge the status quo and redefine the trajectory of knowledge to the people. Scholars do not have to limit themselves. There are limitless activities that would reveal the untapped moral, cultural, academic, and professional interactions which would not only benefit them as individuals but also improve the conditions of the continent beyond expectations. The more we delve into the African past, the more we understand that there are many more things to know, to uncover.

Every generation has its nature-imposed assignment. For the ones who came before us, what they had as an assignment was to place Africa back on the world map of intellectual relevance. To do this, they tirelessly embarked on excavating historical evidence that would validate their claims that Africans had an impressive past and a promising future. Meanwhile, going into this commitment required that they had an instrument to conduct their engagements, but regrettably, they were not equipped with the necessary tools because the environment of action was not theirs. What I mean by this is that they were not especially grounded in the English language the way they were in Yorùbá or their native African languages, and thus, the manipulation or transmission of their findings, thoughts, and intellectual efforts was not done effectively. I measure effective transmission by the ability to make an impact in the world of the Europeans while simultaneously making impressive landmarks in the world of the indigenous people. This was practically impossible, but they achieved a considerably fair victory through what they could achieve, notwithstanding the odds. In our own generation, there are instruments and resources, but the agency of translating these into concrete results that would materialize between the world of the European and that of Africans is a problem, yet scholars are making impressive waves.

The responsibility of this generation is different. I would say that I interpreted it as something that desires a multidisciplinary and transdisciplinary approach. When you look at it critically, scholars who are making names for themselves and, by implication, their places of origin are not adequately equipped to spread the message of Africa's greatness to the world. Those who are, therefore, making the waves are needed to undertake more than the academic responsibility conferred on them by their professional careers. This is important because they are, in most cases, the agencies through which the world sees Africa. This means that the world would only see the aspect of knowledge that they project. Consider, for example, how Chimamanda Ngozi Adichie is making impressive marks for herself, her Western audience would only understand Africa through the lens of her literature. Of course, this, itself, is an addition. However, what I am after is that imagine that the same Ms. Adichie is writing about Africa's medicine, law, and justice, among others, apart from the fact that her audience would begin to understand Africa's perspectives in these areas of knowledge, more information would be easily accessible to scholars about Africa's values in these areas.

This exactly is my motivation to undertake writings and scholarship that are transdisciplinary and, in the same breath, multidisciplinary in approach. The fact that I was trained as a historian has substantially been helpful in this career diversity. Of course, the accumulation of knowledge that lecturers put into us and the underlying circumstances of Africa that introduced us to numerous other experiences gave me the confidence to perform the experiments, which you have seen in my books. It is important to tell you that it has received admirable feedback. More than what could be predicted, there are many scholarly works that are influenced by the writings that we have dedicated our time to exploring in recent times. I cannot deny the obvious fact that the combination of the zeal to make a difference, the undertaking of responsibility to introduce new systems to intensify African mental freedom, and the need to satisfy my innate desire to pioneer great ideas are the cornerstone of my determination. Of course, History as a discipline has helped me significantly in this trajectory. Perhaps, I would not have sustained the tempo to continue if I had started from a different academic background. The shift was considered necessary, and the efforts were easily flowing, not minding the unfolding challenges that come in the process. What has not been contested is the fact that Africa, as a whole, needs this reawakening and that it must happen.

While people think I have demonstrated my fullest intellectual capacity in the writings associated with me from the beginning of my career in writing, I tell in all seriousness that there are more areas, which I have reasonable knowledge capacity, which I am yet to unleash. For instance, my knowledge and dep in economics are things I have not particularly exploited in my writings. I have amassed a great knowledge of economics that when I begin to reel them into books, experts in the field will identify magnificent addition to them in global scholarship. I had dedicated much attention to all these when I was under tutelage, and I must be frank with you, my openness to intellectual engagements has always helped advance my knowledge in any field where I put my attention. As an undergraduate, I experienced many scholarly interactions with books written by experts in the field, which has continued to help me improve what I knew. Although I was married to history as my most preferred area of learning, I gave my time to other areas of academic interest, which I believed would assist me. I read works written by gurus in the field, and from then on, whether overtly or covertly, I continue to devote my time to accumulating knowledge in that field. I have reserved the education I got here for future exploration. When I began to explore them, they would be available for critics and admirers.

I cannot even overemphasize how my academic dexterity in sociology has improved from time immemorial. As I have stated elsewhere, there has been an inseparable connection between some disciplines as they appear to work hand in glove. It is difficult, for example, to be deeply immersed in history and not, for example, to understand an appreciable part of people's sociology. This is informed by the reality that a people's history expands to the area of social systems and how they have continued to operate that particular system for a very long time. The ways that society is programmed in terms of social and cultural traditions would therefore reveal the patterns of their growth concerning the arrangement. This means that having a historical understanding of the African people has substantially improved my knowledge of sociology. Although I am concerned with African history, I have also known of their developmental trajectory through the knowledge of sociology I have gathered. Thus, it is not unexpected that I have produced works considered useful in the field, and the fact is always that there are many other things to put together for intellectual consumption. The development of Africa in all of its dimensions constitutes the knowledge of sociology that I have continued to explore in my intellectual engagement.

In addition, the structure of African society and its functioning forms the part of the knowledge of sociology that I have dished and continued to dish out to my audience. Like every other human society, African society is structured along a line that connects to its philosophy. In essence, a range of groups and identities are always identified in the African environment. There is the king and his subjects. Meanwhile, kingship is a political structure validated by the various African societies, understanding that they shoulder the responsibility of leadership for people in the environment. As powerful as these kings were, they would govern only when they exchanged ideas with their ministers, who were meant to offer different ideas and philosophies in managing a particular area of life. To that extent, a minister of defense, for example, would offer military tactics on how the society would be preserved against external aggressors. This means that such is a social structure and how they dedicate their attention to ensuring the structure's functionality is part of what we understudy in the sociology of the people. Beyond the leadership of a people, there is the breaking down of the community into units, realizable by different family structures available in the society. One can understand the dimensions of economic permutations of a community by merely knowing the family trees in the society.

In creative writing, too, I have begun to explore my talents there. I have relied on the acquired knowledge and extensive reading of vibrant creative writers of Africa to improve myself and then offer educative perspectives to the texts, which are either written by individuals or to interrogate the body of works of these scholars to knowledge production entirely. Knowledge of creative writing is not alien to people who grew up in our generation. For one, ours was still a time when elders, especially the grandparents, took the responsibility of taking us all through the stories of the past and the collective history of the people. I should state here that the communal authorship that resulted in the production of different stories helped shape our childhood as a student of informal creative writing classes. For one, we understood from the series of encounters that we had that humans are capable of being realized as different characters in their engagements. Like the tortoise as the totem of the Yorùbá stories, the human character can also be realized in different attributes and dimensions. Truly, there is always a deep-seated connection between their stories and the conditions of human society. We know several things that are glued to our heads till the contemporary time.

Therefore, understanding the complex interplay of character promiscuity in many African texts became very easy and intellectually stimulating. Since the stories which we listened to as children helped us in many ways to understand the interconnection between the elements of fictional works, setting, plot, characters and characterization, and point of view, among other things, we then know that there are different things to tie the works of arts to in the human society. Looking at the cultural orientations of the African people and their creative ways of introducing them in narratives, I have understood why their creative energy dissipates different contents in their engagements. For this, the concentration on critical evaluation of some 18-h fictional works and sometimes nonfiction that African writers author has been my primary environment of exploration to see how keenly connected the African stories and their various aspects of human experience or history. When looking at the aesthetics of language, one cannot but see how the African literary culture remains a fertile intellectual environment foregrounded by its consummate attributes that are not usually seen in other works. Although I do not think I can write fictional works, for now, the aspect of critical analysis of literary texts has been taken seriously.

Sanya Osha: There is a powerful Pan-Africanist element in your work. Can you discuss the intellectual antecedents to this development and the kind of vision that influenced it?

Toyin Falola: Answer

Every movement in the world begins as a response to a particular experience. Movements are developed from the awareness of people about certain regular experiences that they understand would have a negative effect on them on the occasion that no effort is made to challenge the system. We, therefore, can talk about Communism as an idea and then as a movement, the same way we can talk about the intellectual movement of the Renaissance era, among others. This means that these engagements have come to evolve into a more formidable action group that people make conscious efforts to improve on or, in some cases, preserve. In a sense, this definition makes an implicit conclusion that movements are an integral part of human civilization. As its crucial component, it underscores the process, time, or stage that people get to before they change their story, as the formulation of movement has been globally known as the generator of powerful forces that usually change the course of actions and direction of a people. For Africans, there seems to be a justified reason to create some form of movement for themselves in the unfolding world. One, the experience of political conquest in the hands of European imperialists is generally and totaling in its consequences. This leaves not many African countries off the hook of remote domination.

In addition to this, Africans became victims of cultural genocide in recent history, from about 500 years ago to the present. They experienced, in stark reality, the dehumanizing consequence of humanitarian atrocities committed against them from centuries of revisionist history, defeatist syndrome arising from it, identity politics, mudslinging of their moral and ideological values, condemnation of their historical beliefs, and the perpetual incineration of their intellectual, economic, and social institution to the extent that they were browbeaten into accepting what does not represent them as theirs. This happened to such an extent that the African child is already bequeathed with a dented and broken image that would be working assiduously to undermine him even before his birth. The ones who have been born were unfortunately raised in an environment where the content of their education was drawn from a European perspective handed down specifically with the intention to re-engineer their mindset toward Africa: their identity. Thus, the African child already makes a sworn enemy of their root even before hearing or knowing anything about it. He assumes erroneously that what is called Africa must be oozing out barbarism in great magnitude and must be representative of backward civilization in the amazing perimeter. It must be symbolic of shambolic people with infantile intellectual capacity.

One would notice that the atmosphere is already rigged against the African child, and for him to become proud of his continent and, by implication, his identity, there must be some profound events that would not only change his perspective but also rekindle his spirit, instill in him the genuine feeling of African identity where he would be proud to associate himself with that identity. The Pan-African movement of today focuses on embarking on activities that would rekindle the African spirit on a global scale, to strengthen the bonds of these people of African origin so that they would understand who they are and be proud to associate their engagement with it. This bond will have no respect for geography as it would encourage an outreach of people regardless of their physical location to accommodate themselves as one without sentiment for the part of the continent where they come from. Apparently, such a movement understands for a fact that the history of continent-wide slavery has mandated a need for an indivisible association for all the descendants of theirs who suffered tremendously from this barbaric practice that almost obliviated their origin out of the human world. Whereas this movement has been predated by similar forceful ones, such as the Negritude movement, it has a different tenor.

Pan-Africanism understands that while slavery of the past centuries was a political necessity for the imperialists to accomplish greater economic growth, the events of the capitalist culture of the current world do not indicate that slavery would change anytime soon. Of course, the physical bondage of humans through chains might have had a legal stoppage. Slavery is perpetrated in different ways that cannot be fought, especially when the combined forces are weak. Although other groups of people have experienced the brutal hands of slavery, however, Africans continue to remain victims of their very strange behavior of lacking coordination. Creating a movement of such orientation was a political necessity to enhance their survival. Without making efforts for the advancement of agitation, they would continue to fall victim to the capitalist West that plots their downfall using whatever means available. Although the movement emphasizes the need for the consolidation of African greatness through their return visit to their African origin, it is not rigid in its persuasion. The pioneers are aware that movement and migration are a constant human experience that would continue when and where comfortable. In essence, what was important was not to advocate for complete return; it was to understand what home was about in the first place.

To this extent, the advocacy for returning home is encouraged at the philosophical level. Africans are expected to understand the critical importance of accepting themselves. Meanwhile, accepting themselves begins by identifying with the philosophical constructs of African origin. This definitely would assist them in understanding what their role in the world is and how they can navigate their existence to a rewarding and satisfactory level. We cannot contest the fact that the suppression of Afrocentric ideologies has contributed, essentially, to the displacement of African identity in the world of the moment, as Africans themselves are not only denied access to their identity, they are programmed to detest it in all manner possible. To abandon one's historical identity this way is to single oneself for undeserved subjugation and subduing experiences in the hands of the people who are perpetually seeking their downfall. In essence, Africans are bound by a similar fate which calls for communal actions and collective loyalty in pursuing them. To that extent, Pan-Africanism promises to present them the golden opportunity to fight their fights and be saved as a people or perish as an identity.

To be honest, the movement has birthed quite a number of political institutions that embrace the responsibility to attune Africa as a collective identity with the global community. The Organization of African Unity that metamorphosed into the African Union is an indication and evidence of progress. In all intent and purpose, this body seeks to compel a set of political actions and principles that will, for the most part, handle African affairs for the benefit of all. Through it, intra-African trade will increase and cross-border movements will be facilitated, both of which would bring improvement to the continent as a whole. Whereas this group might not be as formidable as others in terms of the power and influence they wield in determining their safety, they are, nonetheless, making impressive leaps that showcase them as being progressive. Pan-African movement is greater than this, but the fact that they are making great strides is an indication that they are on the right path.

Today, it is not uncommon to find Africans of different cultural origins combining their engagement together and functioning in unison. This, among other things, is evidence that Pan-Africanism is making the right decisions and choices to advance the African worldview. If the sociocultural movement achieved the above-stated goals within the time of engagement, one cannot imagine what adding academic force to it would bring in the long run. I have a role to play, one, as an individual who experienced, firsthand, the negative consequences of removing an individual from his or her cultural and ideological roots, and two, as an African who desires freedom from all its definitions and conception—to be of notable addition to the movement. Even if one refuses to have anything to do with Pan-Africanism, as a scholar, one would be placed in an intellectual quandary in the process for so many reasons. As scholars, especially the ones raised in Africa, one does not have access to the cultural resources from which one would draw for one's intellectual productions. In this case, one is helpless in a sense. For one, you do not have the liberty to weave academic information of other people's origin against which you lack substantial knowledge. And even if you have the access, you need to take a position; it is either you favor the predators in the jungle of scholarship whose writings continually hunt the prey, or you stand firmly by the side of the prey whose access to freedom and self-expression is being usurped by the predator. It is my conviction that staying on the side of Africa would achieve numerous purposes for me.

I envision an African space where people would be free in the real sense of the word, and to achieve that, it does not materialize by mere wishful thinking. One needs to understand the politics of writing and make efforts to direct things in ways that would benefit one's origin and identity. Africans are free only to the extent of breathing. Take breathing away from the equation and you will notice that Africans are not actually free. People who continually run to the other world to seek economic survival, not fulfillment, cannot be said to be free. One cannot adjudge free people who have zero tolerance for their neighbors under the fear they can be persecuted anytime because the said neighbors are nursing the same thoughts. I mentioned "economic survival" and not "fulfillment" to delineate what the people who come to Africa do and what Africans go to other places to do. When you move out of your comfort zone so that you survive and have access to daily meals when you work, you do not seek fulfillment; you seek survival. That exactly is what happens to many Africans in other places. Meanwhile, they have untapped resources that can be converted into results for everyone to benefit. By the combination of leadership ignorance, and greed, the African leaders pay poor attention to the myriad of natural resources, tapping only the ones that can fill their pockets and not satisfy their people. It is the resulting hardship from this senseless engagement that undermines the progress of Africa. Pan-Africanism in this modern day addresses these issues.

Sanya Osha: You are not only a scholar but also a public intellectual who is very concerned about bridging the traditional divide between town and ivory tower. One of your latest initiatives in this regard is the popular TF Interviews. Can you discuss the various motives for this kind of action and thinking?

Toyin Falola: Answer

It occurred to me at a point that the capacity of intellectuals and their potential to transform human society are unlimited. In every sound mind is an arsenal of ideas with unlimited possibilities to change the status quo of their environment for good. Whereas one can only measure these people through their actions when they evaluate that the situations of events are unsuitable for future development. They are those with foresight and the prescient clairvoyance to see what the future would be when a particular set of actions and activities are taken. Unlike others, they understand the importance of decisions and the inevitability of their consequences. In essence, when they understand that a society is moving toward a particular direction, they would immediately evaluate what it would potentially bring to the people and society in the future. If they perceive potential danger, they are always making sacrifices to ensure that the world takes appropriate measures that are considered less risky or less dangerous for humanity. Their lives are used as necessary sacrifices to better the conditions of the world. We would see this in the life of Socrates, a philosopher who, despite his generation's limitations to understand the consequential events of their excessive intermix of religion and politics, continued on his path of truth-telling as his contribution to his generation. He persisted, even when he was resisted. Though what happened to Socrates is evidence of many things, the interpretation is subject to individual sentiment or bias.

For anyone who is a religious apologist, decapitating the philosopher's life through poisoning would have been considered a necessary action to prevent anti-religious individuals from influencing the minds of the innocent majority. However, for someone not tied to religious morals, what Socrates did was deserving of encomium, if not for any other reason, but for the single fact that he offered a fresh perspective from which people could see humanity and the world generally. Apparently, people in the past would have thought about making such changes, but the understanding that the sacrifices it takes to do that would be too much of a luxury that they can afford prevented them from such indulgence. The focus of my argument about this philosophy is not on his efforts against religion and religious politics; it is on the idea that sacrifices are needed to transform an otherwise vulnerable society that has been captured and subjugated by those profiting from misgovernance, misdirection, and mismanagement, which is the case with many African countries. Quite a number of people are benefiting from the present arrangements, and it takes a different level of confidence to challenge it.

If you ask me about bridging the gap between the town and the gown, the question you are asking is inherently affirmative of the understanding that there is actually a gap between the two. If we already have such a reality, the right question would be, "Why is there a separation between the town and the gown, especially when one understands that they have a common goal, and that is the fact of bringing changes to human society?" To answer this latest question, I need to bring you into what happened in my mind recently. I was beginning to look at the African world and immediately saw various divisions. These divisions are not based on philosophical expediency; they are constructed alongside the same area where the colonizers introduced us as Africans. This is why some of us take every business of decolonization very seriously. But I would not particularly highlight what I saw in these African divided spaces—that is better suited in any of my future books. But as a hint, I would refer what happens in the Western world, with which I am equally familiar. Look at the Western world where they import all the forms of instruments we use in Africa (political, ideological, economic, and even spiritual). You have the category of people whom you call the upper class, the middle class, and the lower class. The first category of people under the idea of democracy put in place measures that would render the powerless others vulnerable. The subjugated ones would only be needed when it is time for elections, and they always tilt toward the ones who offer them succor when they are hungry.

Now, more people are "hungry" (in its ideological sense), and when they follow a particular angle of decision, we would generally say it is the choice of the majority. The question is, how then is the majority sound in making these decisions? You would see this is a very complex situation. Mind you, these Western people use the same language to communicate their ideas, exchange economic interactions, conduct their political affairs, and handle their education. Now, imagine what would be the case for us Africans who adopt their ideas but use different languages in our social interactions. Do you not, therefore, see that this division would be more complex and, for that reason, foretell a fearful future for the African people? What I am saying, in essence, is that Africans have imposed the gap between the classes of society. In fact, you would notice too that the credit for that saying goes to Western civilization. In pre-colonial

Africa, there was no town and there was no gown. In other words, the town was the same with the gown, and this helped in enabling inclusivity in political, economic, social, and cultural engagements. But in one way or the other, we have (un)consciously imported the idea of town and gown and the separation it brought to the African space, causing unwholesome damage to our civilization as a people.

You would have noticed by now that what drives my passion in doing TF Interview Series is to first return the African values to their appropriate place. This begins with the recalibration of society into its non-divisive entity that would usher in a new perspective to everything we do. Those who we have unconscientiously removed from the issues that concern their existence would first have a sense of belonging. As researchers, we understand how profound an experiment would be when given all the necessary attention and concentration. This experiment, I must be frank with you, has proved to be a successful one. Beyond what could have been envisaged, we are now getting to know the "insignificant" majority and understand how they view the "decision-making minority." In the past, they have loathed and disagreed with the direction the elites have decided to take their society, and they have begun to react. The irony is that, as elites, we have failed to connect their actions to protest and resistance, but I will show you a few.

The pre-colonial father did not abandon many of his responsibilities for whatever reason, and the pre-colonial mother did not have to nurse fears of exclusion because there were institutions that responded to their cries and answered them. Anything related to moral principles is handled by every member with the awareness that their actions have a greater consequence on society. Today, people don't just care about these things.

Although what I have done is a surface-scratching effort aimed at restoring the values that are inadvertently eroding the African sociopolitical and sociocultural pace in the name of creating a gap where none existed. If you asked me if the separation is necessary to keep the sanity of the academic community intact, I would tell you that such an approach is merely evasive. It is avoiding the greater looming danger, some of which we are seeing gradually in contemporary times. There are ways to indicate if society is measurable along the lines of people's access to education or not. When it is done haphazardly as the current schools of African scholars are doing, there will come a time when the danger would be completely invertible. The primary concern is to interrogate the crucibles of the intellectual property locked in the minds of the ones we call gowns. They are invited into our space to understand and begin to reshape their views about life by juxtaposing things on their own. Although the platform you have alluded to has been in existence for some time now, it has achieved a commendable result in its relative recency. One of the things we have achieved with it is bringing together a community of scholars who are mainly of African progeny and are located in different countries of the world. These scholars have gained an understanding of what different societies are and how their organization contributes to the conditions they find themselves in, not only through the reading of texts but also through firsthand experience. As African scholars in the diaspora, we have been able to spread the influence of Pan-African identity to bring intelligent minds together so that we can benefit from their critical ideas that would bring value to everyone. What is sacrosanct here is that the physical bridge erected by the nature of human geography has collapsed for very obvious reasons. There existed a form of difference among scholars of different academic disciplines and career landscapes, making it impossible for them to join forces for common advantage.

With the power of technology, we have harvested fermented intellectual properties of many African scholars who come to our space and discuss several things. We have invited scholars who are passionate about Afrocentric legitimacy and de-escalation of colonial structures that have re-engineered the cognitive system of the African people. At the appropriate time, they educated us on why the various areas of Africa's political, social and economic life have continued to experience their shadow selves. Through them, we have learned that the combinatorial contributions of colonization, neocolonialism, and excessive assimilation of Western ideas have sterilized the African systems and made them vulnerable to external manipulations, aggressions, and threats. These educated fellows bond together and, like us, are also beginning to see how the importance of maximizing opportunities presented by technology and the media is almost inexhaustible. Rather than divert their energies to wrong activities or engagements of zero cultural and political advantages, they have continued to see why it is commonsensical to come together under the same umbrella to rejuvenate dying African spirits and restore their dignity. Gradually but steadily, we are creating a social hub where everyone considered intellectually fertile, irrespective of their town or gown status, would be brought to our space for an interview. We would be able to learn from them and identify with their perspectives as much as they demonstrate a good knowledge of their topic. We do not deserve a continent divided for reasons we don't know. Most of the challenges we face as a people become enduring because we do not articulate them in most cases. We would not even know that many of our problems can be immediately resolved when we talk about them to one another. If we continue to underplay the importance of communication, we will keep the suppressive structures erected by the European imperialists and give them the power to divide us. If we are scholars, we should understand the benefit of making use of every opportunity that presents itself to us. If past Africans organized continent-wide actions and agitations that won them independence and international recognition at a time when there was no internet or social media, this current generation has no excuse not to do exceedingly better. We need to take advantage of the virtual space that offers us the opportunity to interface across borders, interact across countries, and interchange ideas across nations. We are making impressive landmarks in that trajectory already.

Sanya Osha: You are renowned for your consistent collaborative projects drawing together scholars of diverse backgrounds and orientations. In fact, this aspect of your work is almost philosophical in nature and also of an evident activist tendency. Again, what are the explanations for this approach?

Toyin Falola: Answer

This particular question is somewhat connected to the previous one, but to avoid the monotony of information, I will answer this in a more relatable way. The first thing that should come to one's mind when in an academic domain or profession is making an impact. In essence, academics should ask themselves if they are ready to make an impact, name, or money. These three things are naturally different. Someone can make an impact without making a name or money for themselves. Even if the name would come, it may come as a posthumous reward. Consider Galileo in this context. His contribution to the understanding of physics on how the Earth revolves around the Sun was a monumental scientific milestone that made him have an impact in that field but did not fetch him a good reputation at the time of discovery. Rather than being recognized for that intellectual feat, he was persecuted. Regardless of the fate they meted on him in his generation, the impact this single discovery encouraged in physics is still felt in contemporary times. That is an impact. I don't also think it fetched him the money to commensurate the said discovery. However, many also make a name for themselves but not an impact. Saddam Hussein of Iraq, in my estimation, is a good example of someone who made a name for himself but not an impact in the moral sense of it. He is remembered as an Eastern individual who confronted the West to stop them in their tracks of imposition. But how did this impact or give him money? The example of people who make money but not name or impact are everywhere in this capitalist economy of the contemporary time. So, it is pointless to reiterate it. I am indirectly saying that for academics, especially, it is important that they ask themselves what they want to be in all these shortlisted possibilities. It is possible to do all, to be candid. However, it is equally possible to get tempted along the line if one does not define what one wants to be. Therefore, to make an impact requires more than an individual's capacity. Apart from the folly inherent in trying to do a four-man's job, a foreman cannot excellently execute the assignment meant for four different people. Collaboration is, therefore, a necessity and also an important instrument for achieving efficiency. Toyin Falola, no matter how eclectic he is, cannot have a similar impact he would have when joined in actions and activities with another set of people.

In essence, it is a mark of mental strength to understand one's natural limitations and identify how helpful collaboration with others would be. For example, I am from Nigeria and I am familiar with the cultural terrain of that country. This privilege comes from being an active member of the Nigerian community and an academic who has done innumerable research engagements about the place. However, I know Addis Ababa as a country of progressive African people that should be explored and appreciated. Of course, I have a community of scholars there too. But I would not make as much impact on an Ethiopian, especially when it comes to driving academic or cultural ideas into them, as much as the most popular Ethiopian writer would do. In essence, one will see that it is just a matter of intellectual prudence to collaborate with such colleagues if truly I am interested in making an impact. Ego does not bring people results. In fact, rather than ensure that an individual is up and doing, ego collapses their capacity and makes a mockery of whatever they are doing. It is in this thinking that I, for one, consider collaboration as a strength rather than the opposite. Although people's perspectives would vary, I find someone who can sacrifice their ego and bring brains together more important and instrumental to development than an individual who can do a workaholic job by himself. The Yorùbá people have a saying that reveals the folly in that orientation, and I will paraphrase it. They say that any indulgence that one rejects younger people from participating in would imminently perish. Therefore, if knowledge production is conceived as an indulgence and the African people are not making efforts to co-opt others into doing it, they would soon run out of intellectual excellence through exhaustion. Thus, I see the process of bringing others together as an avenue to keep the system alive and agile. That would save Africans from a number of things. Similarly, humans are, by nature, designed to be limited. Anyone who interrogates the ways of nature very deeply would understand that nature is uninterested in human's boundless capacity. The most basic way to arrive at this point is to evaluate human physical properties. When we stretch our hands or expand our other anatomical properties, we would see that the instant sphere of our influence is within the space where we can reach. Nature does not offer man the opportunity to have beyond that influence; otherwise, man would have been everywhere at the same time like oxygen. Provided a man can do more, he would perhaps have been dismissive of others' influence in bringing change. Evidently, both Jesus and Mohammed of the two faiths that have the largest population need others to expand their religious ideologies. In essence, the need for multidisciplinary collaboration is underscored by different reasons. Africans and the world must come to the awareness that their intellectuals are on the same page. Since what is important to us is to make an impact, neither the language others speak does matter, nor is the religion they profess an important thing. The possibility that they can offer the world a better understanding and perspective should be the basis of our relationship. We have been doing this for a long time.

Getting along with other scholars is my way of expressing a commitment to revolutionizing the African intellectual space, where we adopt new systems and approaches to the challenges that are staring us in the face. From Kenya to Uganda, Namibia to Sierra Leone, Ethiopia to Ghana, Cameroon to Togo, Nigeria to South Africa, and Tanzania to Mozambique, there is a fair deposit of African scholars who have substantial intellectual resources they want to offer us. The underlying advantages of these things are numerous. In the course of collaboration, I have discovered that there are perspectives to knowledge that would not be known in the absence of such unity. And more importantly, the reception that one has in other African countries comes from the understanding that I make bold collaborations with scholars and game changers who continue to expand my name where I physically have never been to. Invariably, they too become the bride of my audience, who becomes fascinated by the intellectual promises these people show. In the future, one will understand the essence of such sacrifices we make today. For instance, we discover later that the presence of margin between many African countries is inspired by the absence of works that their past intellectuals often did together. However, the current collaboration would change the narrative for good.

I answer the other side of your question that addresses my part of intellectual activism by mentioning again that everything boils down to what people decide to do with their lives. Name is a very important thing among the Yorùbá people. If anything, they are always reminded of how important it is to keep a good name for themselves and their offspring for future occasions. As much as I already have the mindset to make an impact, what is next is how I decide to achieve that goal. It is important because setting goals is generally easy for everyone. However, the possibility of achieving these goals is uncertain since people usually do not match their thinking and wishes with actions in whatever way. Now, here is where I make the difference. If have the ambition to become instrumental to Africa's transformative development by offering intellectual services that would reposition people's perspectives and guide them right in their decision-making, I had better devise a stronger approach to achieving the ambition or forget it.

This is where activism comes in as a firebrand approach to achieving that potential. One, the people against whom your intellectual productions are targeted so that they would inspire generational good and actions enough to challenge the status quo and channel their energies aright are irrevocably intransigent. They have mastered the way of pretense and would always mastermind backward actions that would frustrate the efforts of the government and individuals to achieve greatness; therefore, to apply a calm approach would be counter-productive. Apparently, they are unbothered by the discomfort of the masses and would not budge if the common people undergo series of unbearable challenges. As a result, one must take a position, even from the intellectual productions one is making, as there is no in-between. There is the temptation to identify with the significant minority as they are always ready to offer everything that would bring about comfort and relief to the person. However, identifying with them would mean being an accessory to all forms of destructive engagements carried out against the powerless in the community.

Knowing that the subaltern deserves the recognition they need and understanding their plight has a way of compelling one to identify with them. Remember that I discussed briefly what is necessary to humans in a previous revelation. One would have to choose between having names or not having them. One does not make a good name by defending the oppressors as that would have never-ending consequences on the harmless people. Against this background, I have used my works to challenge the bourgeoise while I employed my platform to tackle the oppressors at the superstructure level who make every effort to frustrate the capabilities, efforts, and contributions that ordinary people have made in society. Some people have noticed that I appear stern with ideas and positions that I take, which is apparently informed by the commitment to take a position in the events of things. My intellectualism is formed based on an awareness that acceptable moral principles, conventions, and codes should be emphasized across every region so that individuals would not be victims of jaundiced inequity manifested in a poor justice system, unequal access to wealth, and warped education system.

This has dominated my writing to the extent that even when I write history, it is usually difficult to deny its advocacy for a particular course of action. While I persuade in most of my works, I also ensure they speak truth to power without coercing them on the ideas we have brought out. Meanwhile, I am not a lone wolf. I did not embark on this journey riding on the assumption that everyone would accept me. I have continued to hold my position, identify those with a similar line of reasoning, and combine our efforts to produce desirable and anticipated results. People from different academic fields have seen the overwhelming beauty inherent in collaboration and a multidisciplinary approach to scholarship. In the course of our combined activism, we have uncovered various issues underpinning African underdevelopment and, in some cases, come up with solutions that would bring effective solutions to the highlighted challenges. Most of our positions have been pushed as statements of policies to different governments in Africa, and because they understand that we have intellectual brilliance, they, in most cases, respect what we do and how we are changing the narratives of Africa in Africa itself and beyond its shores.

Sanya Osha: For over 30 years, you have been based in North America. How has this location impacted your views on the study of Africa? Would you say it has brought you closer to the continent or driven you farther away?

Toyin Falola: Answer

I was over 30 when I moved to North America to continue my career. Spending more than three decades in Africa with firsthand experience of the African cultural space qualifies one to be called a true African, no matter the metric used to arrive at a conclusion. What I am saying, in essence, is that I had a strong understanding of what Africa was during my stay in Nigeria, and my knowledge was consolidated by the accumulation of ideas from different sets of intellectuals intermixed with the information acquired informally. To argue against my deep-seated immersion in Africa's cultural traditions and political involvement is an exercise in futility. Although one cannot understand everything about a people's cultural and historical experience, understandably because there are always angles that evade the most brilliant observer while giving a detailed account of incidences of the past. To this extent, I would accept that there were things I did not have reliable knowledge about with regard to African history, but I can say with authority that many things about the continent have been in my intellectual arsenal since the time I referenced it. Moving to America introduced other different, interesting dimensions to my knowledge of Africa and myself. It may sound surreal, but that is the case.

While we were undergraduate students, nearly all the available written materials about Africans were documented by Europeans or Western apologists. By this condition, we were left to the politics of social and mental re-engineering that pervaded the intellectual world of those who came before us.

There has always been a nauseating danger in allowing an external individual unaffected by issues that concern one's existence to document one's history. In fact, no matter how good-willed the person is, it is just a matter of emotional bias, and he would succumb to the temptation to misrepresent you. Sometimes they do this out of sheer envy, and sometimes, they do it out of conscientious ignorance. Where people of goodwill write your stories and are prone to manipulating or distorting events, how much more are the people who are fixated on weaponizing intellectualism against you? I grew up reading Immanuel Kant, whose eternal disarticulation of African history remains very direct, showcasing his disgust for Black people and whatever is associated with them. I was equally reading Trevor-Roper, whose account of African history is nothing short of beguiling and assassinating in outlook. I read literary fiction authored by Western writers, and I would, like everyone else, conclude that Africa and Africans were, apart from deserving to be invaded by these Western expansionists, truly barbaric, uncivilized, and acutely primitive. But the access I had to books that offered counter-arguments always gave me the balance. Please, note that if what was written by the European writers and their Western apologists were meant to malign the African people and strip them of any dignity and decency, we can comfortably identify tenors of their writing as racist. Also, bear in mind that most of these scholars barely knew Africa or its diverse cultural traditions and ideological landscapes. Aside from their anthropological ignorance, they imposed narratives on the African people and continued in that destructive engagement for a long time. Imagine that one finds himself in an academic environment, political atmosphere, or social setting where such works that are associated or linked to the scholars mentioned earlier were considered a game, what manner of indignity do you think such an individual would suffer? I'll leave you to do the arithmetic. The fact that I was away in a different environment, a Western one, made me realize my color pigmentation. While in Nigeria, I traveled from one part of the country to another on several occasions, but it never, at any point in time, occurred to me to be conscious of the color of my skin. No matter the size of hospitality in North America, the fact that you would naturally see yourself as of a different skin color prepares you for potential racist encounters. You would be in expectation that someone would mention this difference in skin color or hair texture to you at the slightest opportunity. And, of course, that is how humans are naturally programmed to take notice of differences. By my awareness of the difference in my skin color, not necessarily by any racist experience, I became more interested in learning about Africa. Perhaps, the urge to learn is innate in every person, but the commitment to learn is more dominant in those who are naturally curious. The basis for that new interest was an assumption that if someone deliberately invests in distorting the histories of others, sensible people should strive to understand what these vested interests are trying to hide from the public because in there lies the truth about the same subject. You do not invest heavily in assassinating the character of a proven criminal. The available evidence would always do the job. When it gets to the level of investing one's resources into making a supposed criminal look bad, something is usually fishy. Observing these trends enabled me to begin to acquaint myself even more with works by Americans and also world history for two reasons. One, I wanted to study more American literature to understand the cornucopia of values about Africa that was truly misrepresented. It is important for sophisticated countries like America to invest in reputation management of itself to gain more love and affection from the wider world. But I usually think ahead, and as such, I am not easily swayed by superficial rhetoric. Second, I needed to study the history of America firsthand so that I would understand the roles the Black Man played in its evolution. This was informed by the understanding that getting such information would lead me to make a connection between the perpetual downplaying of Africa's historical greatness and the desire to continue dominating them in the emerging global capitalist culture. To my amazement, it would be discovered that the African people made irrefutable contributions to the advancement of America and, by extension, all Western civilization. To downplay the contributions that Africa made, it was a matter of political necessity to invest in narratives that undermined the people in every sense of the word. Of course, I cannot change what America decides to do with its power and political influence. However, as a global citizen, I knew I could change how the perspectives of the African people were reconstructed, re-engineered, and recalibrated to accommodate the thoughts that a punctured history is a deliberate orchestration of some vested interests against which they are free to resist and challenge any of such thing that undermines their honor.

I had only one avenue to do that, and that was through writing. The fact that I write a lot finds credence in the understanding that I have quite a lot of things I wish to tell my audience. More than the superficial appreciation of African history, I became involved in unveiling deeply rooted African history that cuts across the two sides of the binary prism. Since the new status afforded me an opportunity to dine with decision makers, I realized that as much as the West continued to undermine the greatness of Africa, these Westerners were actually assisted by various categories of Africans who made themselves available as accomplices to be used for the distortion of the African history, the displacement of African values and the contamination of the African ideologies. What I have said here is that I have moved from being a distant observer of the African situation even though I was in Africa to being a closer viewer of events with access to more important information to shape my knowledge. To be candid, my movement to North America helped me substantially in knowing Africa more realistically and deeply than my education as an undergraduate student afforded me, even though it was the foundation on which the latter stood. I have moved on from being a distant observer in the activities of Africa to being an active participant in its remodeling and rejuvenation.

If you ask me whether this incidence of movement has drawn me closer to the continent or has driven me far away from it, I would answer you by drawing practical examples that would provide you with a clear-cut answer. I cannot count the number of programs and projects, among others, that I have facilitated in different African countries for the past three decades since I left the continent. It would even be misleading to say that I left Africa in the practical sense. I shuttle between the continent and other parts of the world in a bid to introduce values, ideas, and opportunities and contribute very immensely to the advancement of the continent's collective development. I have been involved in organizing conferences and workshops, symposia, and platforms where issues that relate to Africa are thrashed and discussed. The Toyin Falola Conference (TOFAC) is an academic platform where we allow academics to come together and showcase what they have been doing in their careers in terms of research and scholarship. This has always created the environment for the enhancement of exchanges of ideas where people add to what they have already known and also exchange contacts to advance their individual careers.

I have facilitated scholars' movements to the continent too. These scholars educate the people in many dimensions on many important things with regard to their environment, life, politics, civic responsibility, cultural, and even religious discourses. These individuals have substantially used the platforms to increase their own participation in African-related engagements. We have organized peace accords with warring factions in various African countries and offered policy advice to many others in the continent that need to be attuned to the emerging realities of the world. We have also provided scholarship opportunities to people. We have built platforms where we pay the education fees of students and also offer them opportunities to meet with one another as budding African scholars. The majority of these beneficiaries have continued to make outstanding changes in their own individual lives. In whatever ways possible, we have always made efforts to alleviate the challenges that people face, not because it is their fault, but primarily because they are Africans. It becomes very emotional when it is discovered that many talents are left unattended in Africa over the reality that many people abandon them and condemn them to fate. You would see from the various highlights above that I have been drawn closer to the continent more than you could possibly have imagined. Although my physical component might be in North America, I cannot understate how connected I have been to Africa since the beginning of my journey as a scholar. In fact, I tell you the reality when I say that I have access to some events that happen on the continent before some of the people living there. I would not tell you that all we have achieved have been without corresponding hostile challenges. We have faced situations where our commitment was tested, our dedication overstretched, and our spirit crushed by forces that do not want these things to happen to or in Africa and for Africans. And you would have noticed my use of the first-person plural pronoun "we" in this engagement. This is practically because I am not self-made. I flourish because some people offered me their shoulders to stand on while others practically drew me along to make these astronomical impacts. Africa is always in me. I have always nursed the ambition to be instrumental to its development, and I am happy to be a notable one in its recent history. The realization that I am in a different country does not erase the fact that I am deeply connected to my root. North America has offered me many things, and I am forever appreciative of that rare opportunity. We are who we are because of the circumstances that shape us.

Sanya Osha: You are the holder of at least four traditional chieftaincy titles. What aspect of your activities do you think has endeared to traditional authorities? In some of our private conversations, you revealed some of the values and lessons you learnt from traditional elders. Would you care to share some of them in this forum?

Toyin Falola: Answer

Attracting chieftaincy tittles among the Yoruba people comes from two different developments: one, your lineage, which is hereditary, and two, your outstanding contributions to humanity, which shows efforts or dedication of selflessness. Interestingly, the system has survived many ages so much that one would always expect that the suitability of an individual for a chieftaincy position is borderline hereditary. Although I should not forget to remind you that in almost all the places, and among the Yoruba people, some chieftaincy positions are strictly ceremonial by which condition they are mere fanciful roles that people receive for their social impact performances, while at the same time, others are for critical sociopolitical and even socioeconomic values as in my case. The beneficiaries have access to the most important discourses in the community since they hold a germane stake in the community. For the former, the beneficiary can come from a different cultural background and be rewarded with titles as a recognition of their humanitarian services that they want others to emulate. By conferring such people with chieftaincy titles, the benefactor uses the roles to send an important message to others about the inherent advantages of being good and also being instrumental to the wellness of society.

The people who are rewarded with this recognition would, in turn, function effectively to improve the social network of the community by exploiting their social popularity to attract development to the society that gave them such recognition. This is the reason nearly all the wealthy people in many African countries have one chieftaincy or the other to their names. In most cases, they are expected to invite the people in their social ring to come with investment into the said community so that they would assist in the socioeconomic development of the place. It may interest you to note also that the conferment of titles in this way is sometimes done as conflict prevention or resolution strategy to enhance development for the people. The Yorùbá people are a foresighted group, and they demonstrate their outstanding intellectual capacity for societal control through their actions and even inactions. In an urban and multicultural community, due to trade relationships that have sparked some level of movements across borders, the Yorùbá people could identify groups by conferring titles to some of them so that they would continue to maintain peaceful relationships and avoid altercations in future relationships. This has helped to prevent baseless wars among them and brought about the peace they usually enjoy. I can tell you that some of my chieftaincy titles serve this purpose, especially.
As much as the above submission consolidates the understanding that some settlements in the Yorùbá world adhere to the highlighted practice, there are some special Yorùbá communities that operate on a different level of democratic ideology with their chieftaincy culture or system. While we have identified that some of these titular positions are hereditary, we have as well indicated that some are rewards for the various outstanding contributions that an individual has made in their career or in advancing humanity. In Ibadan, chieftaincy titles follow a different democratic culture. When you are offered a chieftaincy title in Ibadan, what they have indirectly told you is that you are a potential leader of that community of people. In fact, you stand a chance of being king of that settlement if the rotational

system favors you. In Ibadan, people who are offered this reward are believed to possess very impressive characteristics that are required for the advancement of their society. Politicians of important virtue, businessmen and women of outstanding ideals, academics of notable industry, among other areas in their web of recognition over the understanding that they would someday use their ingenuity to bring development to the place. In essence, I am a king in the making. But when we say that people recognize those who make outstanding contributions to their society, what do we mean?
I am an illustrious son of Ibadan, for example, and in all modesty, my strides in the world's academic circle have catapulted me to places where I have never been physically and neither envisaged. Believe me when I tell you that I was in awe of their magnanimity when I received the message that I would be conferred a chieftaincy title. It would have made no difference for anyone who has been working consciously to achieve that feat. This is because such would have been the effort of their hard work, and since they were consciously aiming at it, and it would not have come as a surprise when they achieved it. In my own case, however, I was overwhelmed for many reasons. One, it is a mark of a great job which I think I have been doing since the beginning of my career. For one, you feel that people actually cannot unsee the aura which you ooze through your engagements, as it is evident that without their awareness, you would not be recognized. Two, you would immediately begin to understand that your dedication to academic involvement and participation has come to be of positive impact in the long run because, I must admit, pursuing academic dreams in an environment like Nigeria is a pure gamble. Apart from the general disgust for teachers and researchers since people cannot directly connect them to any important societal stride, the system makes it especially difficult for them on many grounds. Teachers can never compete with many other career professionals in Nigerian society except if they are duplicitous or diabolical. To be recognized with one strong chieftaincy title means a whole lot to me.

If I told you that there was a regimented activity that an individual must follow to attract such a reward, I would be lying to you. I was just myself, striving to be better, to outdo who I was some years earlier. I honestly think that is the basis of success—not going into competition with anyone. I did not see it coming, and I cannot outline what I did to attract the rewards and claiming to know how it worked would be inaccurate. The thing that cannot be denied, however, is that I have continued to demonstrate the trait of a warrior on a battlefield of intellectualism. Without sheathing my sword when faced with challenges of life in the battleground of knowledge seeking and production, I have continued to triumph just like the proverbial warlords of Ibadan origin. While they demonstrated their outstanding capacity in the area of war, I have continued to show my undaunted ability in the academic world. While I cannot specifically say when they got endeared to my works, I, however, cannot remove the fact that the reason for that recognition was my immeasurable contributions in the first place. The situation is, therefore, one that does not rid people of their rights. Once you demonstrate your greater values in whatever field you find yourself in, you will actually be recognized at the appropriate time. After all, the recognition I got must have been signaled by those who had access to my works and were, in a way keeping tabs on my success. I have a feeling that it was these sets of people who suggested me to the authorities for the conferment of the reward.

In essence, to talk about how this has generally influenced my perspective is to open another book of history and conversation that may not be contained in this limited space. In other places where the chieftaincy title was conferred on me apart from Ibadan, the expectation was already known and would remain the basis of our unwritten contract. I call chieftaincy positions unwritten contracts because there are some sets of things that would be expected of you as an individual. In the case that you do not satisfy these preconditions, the expiration of your relevance would be announced, not by stripping you of the title, but by paying less social attention to you. That is the beauty of the Yorùbá world. In essence, to these people, I always ensure I meet their expectations by yielding to their invitations when they come up, and in some cases, I facilitate academic programs that would directly or indirectly benefit them. However, as much as they expect such a level of responsibility from the awardee, they also fulfill their own side of the contract. Many people do not usually know this. In fact, rather than understand the mutuality of their responsibilities, some people who are awarded such recognition believe it is a monodirectional thing. For my grip on the Yorùbá worldview, I know that if you move closer to the traditional leaders, there is a lot of information you would have access to that would add to you as an individual.

One of the unforgettable lessons I have acquired from the elders in these places is that people remain interconnected with one another. Apparently, you would understand that this knowledge is basic, such that one can grab it at an elementary stage of life. However, there is more to it. The interconnectivity of things in the world is underscored by the natural reliance that creatures have on one another to survive. Elders have made me understand more that humans are elements of natural forces and life and every other being that exists in there; their actions and activities have ways by which it affects and, by implication, it determines the events of the world. For instance, someone who is in the custody of the government, serving time, would not understand the implication of the momentary disappearance from other people around. Whereas in not dying, which is their complete disappearance from the face of the Earth, they reserve the opportunity to partake in people's activities of people, albeit in different dimensions. For the most obvious one, people would either appreciate their absence or celebrate it, all depending on the impact that is associated with the individual in context. Such would serve as a lesson to the individual and would make him understand that there is more to life than they have seen, and when they have their freedom undisturbed, they will treasure it. In an environment where they are new, they would cause a number of things to change in the arrangement of their events. This shows the interconnection of life in some ways.

Most of the places where I was recognized with chieftaincy titles are in Yorùbáland, and this has brought me closer to some ideas and values of the Yorùbá people. I have learnt, among other things, that the Yoruba people are essentially calculative and purposeful in all of their engagements. Their liberal nature is underscored by the understanding that people are needed to accomplish some greater things in life. This indicates that one needs to open oneself to external visitation, only that one would have to apply commonsense in doing so. They have educated me that the idea of border-crossing is natural because, through it, intercontinental ideas and intercultural philosophies would be exchanged for the enhancement of competition and progress. Contrary to the misconception that the Yorùbá people are meek and timid, they are actually strong in their foresighted capacity to predict the future and, in a way, make efforts to make it a better place for everyone. One would notice that nearly all Yoruba communities are filled with visitors who use their resources, both intellectual and human, to assist in the advancement of these places, one way or the other. It cannot be overemphasized that they are a people of uncommon tolerance and the zeal to improve their sociopolitical conditions by striving to make them better by all means possible. I have learned that hard work and dedication are very good as they get rewarded with results. I have always believed that people who dedicate themselves to particular courses do not always achieve their aims at the end. But that was because my definition of achievement was limited. I have received more education from them to shift this thought pattern.

Sanya Osha: Do you think your scholarship is being received globally in the appropriate kind of light? Or would you say that you are viewed differently in different parts of the world?

Toyin Falola: Answer

This question is in two directions. The way we define if our productions are being accepted or appropriated differs considerably. First and foremost, I am fundamentally a historian. By this status, my works are generally expected to be appropriated anywhere in the world as the work of a historian. This means that I am particularly interested in making an impact along that line of the academic profession, and my writings have continued to showcase my dedication to that ambition. In essence, a historian's focus is to see the world from a specific perspective so that they would attune their intellectual productions to suit the focus that they have identified. In my own case, I am an African historian, and one of my priorities is to relay the African historical experience in a profound scholarship which would create anticipated awareness in the minds of the people. As an African historian, the world is naturally rigged against you before you begin your engagement. For instance, you would have to strive essentially in the already contaminated atmosphere where the Eurocentric historians have maligned and assaulted the great personality of the African people. To be candid, the vast responsibility above an African historian is indicated by the number of efforts they would have to make to right the wrongs that have been created against them by the West. It is no coincidence that many African historians choose to avoid a number of things.

Not having access to the necessary financial resources with which one would conduct research works places the researcher at a very great disadvantage. You would have to struggle to have access to the necessary resources which would be deployed in conducting one's intellectual exercise. In a case where the individual does not have a ready source to sponsor such lofty ambition, they are limited in their options. For those who are irrevocable in their commitment yet do not have the necessary resources, the most available option they take is to commit their own financial capacity to the dream. Meanwhile, working in Africa as a historian already makes the journey turbulent for you as a teacher and then as a researcher. Consider, for example, that the most populous Black nation in the world, Nigeria, has removed History as a subject from its educational curriculum for elementary school goers and the ones at the high school level. Teachers who are in this line of profession are already at a disadvantage. This is inevitable because they would have limited job opportunities where they can earn a living. If the ones who have attained this level of academic exposure face such treatment, it would be difficult to encourage the up-and-coming generations to settle for such professional choices. By that condition, the historian is hunted and history is hounded.

Beyond the complex intricacies of knowledge acquisition and production that surround History as a discipline, there is the predatory environment where it is already disfavored by various political and cultural issues. African historians are not respected on their own home front. They face stiff resistance in the global community. Their problems are not unconnected to the challenges of all Western permutations that have made it almost impossible to eradicate the litany of embarrassment and abuse to which they have been subjected. Nearly three-quarters of the world believe in the Western story that the history of Africans is the history of Europeans in Africa. To have this understanding means that one is already programmed to challenge any academic material that seeks to validate African epistemology through history. The world is already conditioned to see the efforts of African historians as merely an attempt to score cheap political points by trying to challenge those sentiments of the West which are already frozen in their works. This means that even when you get the necessary resources to gather your ideas together, you would, in most cases, not get the attention of the deserving audience that needs your information to affirm or refute the claims that they have seen before.

Believe me when I say that when you look at the combined efforts of these African historians in the world, they have been nothing short of outstanding and different. We should remember that the assignment for each generation of scholars differs, and it is in identifying the ones that go in line with the generation's focus that one sets out the strategy with which one would achieve the ambition. If the in-house Africans are denied opportunities to learn history, to a considerable extent, they would still be exposed to informal information about their history, which would open them to a number of things that they would need to know. But not having access to Africa's history is an intellectual luxury that other people around the world cannot afford. This is essentially underpinned by the sheer need to correct the backlog of the misconception that they already have about Africans through the works of European authors. For example, anyone but Africans naturally has a negative image of what the people are in the continent. In fact, many Westerners believe that Africa is one country in itself. The many misconceptions of the people about Africa cannot be underplayed. For the most part, they are indeed convinced that Africans are barbaric, primitive, outrageous, and unrefined, and it would be suicidal to get involved in anything with them. The only people to change this wrong impression are the historians, and that is what we are doing.

Consequently, the striving African writer has a truckload of responsibility. As much as the writer is striving to correct the negative impression about Africa in the world, he would be faced with the responsibility to improve his own financial status too. We have not talked about how we face daring circumstances in the hands of publishers. Even the ones that would accept to publish your work, they are always afraid of the market and whether the commercial values would be encouraging. If publishers are not interested in your works, the level of your intelligence and intellectual energy would not matter. Everything you produce would always receive no attention. Meanwhile, your economic growth would be determined by the recognition you get from the audience who reads your works. The success of one's work depends on how vast and fast the wider world gets associated with your works. All these are the forces that you have to deal with as a historian.

I have not mentioned how the academic system of the world is rigged against you. I remember the hurdles and strives that the likes of Kenneth Onwuka Dike, Bolanle Awe, and J. F. Ade Ajayi, among others, went through by arguing that they would appropriate oral sources as the foundation of the history of Africa. They did not only attract derision from the global West communities, but also became the direct victims of blackmail. This continued for a long time and the people remained unapologetic in their convictions. These historians resisted the pressure, persisted, and persevered until the canonization of the oral materials as reliable sources of the people's history. If every human society preserved its history orally before the discovery of orthographical means, how then would it be logical to deny others that right when they argue it would help them trace their remote past in better ways? You would see through these actions that the world is already rigged against African writers, and it is understandable that they experience whatever they are confronted with. Interestingly, we have passed this stage, and it is evident that my works, just as the works of every other African historian, are accepted across the African continent and their various communities. There is also an international acceptability to our works as the evidence lies in how many places where a work is read.

Since your question is centered on me and my works specifically, I would say that how I am viewed cannot be specifically stated. Apparently, I am a historian, but I have graduated to writings that have an affinity with my other academic disciplines. By this condition, I can only be seen from the angle of my works that people are reading. For example, I have written an auto-ethnographical work while I have documented biographies too. In essence, people who pick these materials to read can view me from the perspective of a literary scholar, and they would not be wrong. This is necessary because there are many literary maneuvers that come into play when documenting such experiences. There are others who, for example, have read my works that are written on the Yorùbá metaphysics, and it is not impossible that the audience with background knowledge in theology would view this from the angle of religion, and they too, in my opinion, would not be wrong. I have written many works around migrations and dispersals, which have given me readership in diaspora and transnational studies, and these people understand my works from their own lens. While it would be professionally accurate to refer to TF as a historian, it would, however, not be giving details of him when you consider the eclecticism of his writings. My works are the basis of the plurality of views that people have about me in various parts of the world. Alternatively, others have seen me from the angle of my humanitarian services. I have helped many individuals, and it is understandable when they admire me and celebrate those outstanding things that I brought to them or to their doorstep. I cannot be economical with such fact that there are many detractors who view my works from the angle of envy. To these people, they are always interrogating how I continue to dedicate myself to this calling despite my age. These people, apparently, view me differently. They read my works with a different mindset and intention to maul my integrity. The intensity with which they do this is summarized by their condemnation of things that I do. I am aware of them, and I do not hold them in contempt because they hold this positively. Humans naturally envy others who make more progress where they struggle. However, they have also been useful to me in many ways than can be imagined. Their positions have enabled me to refine my ideas and improve on the areas where I lag behind. All these are the reflections of the intricacies around this involvement of mine.

Sanya Osha: Can you discuss the life and influence of Leku, (and others like her) whom you write about enticingly in *Mouth Sweeter than Salt*, on you as a person and your community?

Toyin Falola: Answer

Every woman and man in the Yorùbá cultural landscape is a body of epistemic and ontological awareness, and they use their knowledge to effect changes in the human world, regardless of where they are. Leku in *A Mouth Sweeter than Salt* is an imposing character in my life; her participation in it fits into what the Yorùbá people call Àyànmó. The closest epistemic idea of Àyànmó in the Western world is destiny, but in the deeper Yorùbá worldview, Àyànmó is an umbrella term for other important phenomena with which they are closely connected for spiritual and supernatural assignments. Given the realization that Leku is a reference point to the Yorùbá's ontological structure of the people, I will make some effort to situate her contributions that underpin my life's experiences from childhood to the present moment. But before I do this, I would not mind to reiterate the importance of communal togetherness in the Yorùbá world and how it helps determine the eventual consequences for every member of society. Togetherness in that cultural landscape is a given and not specifically required by individuals—it is what they do habitually. However, it is a code that comes with consequences on the occasion that an individual refuses to prioritize it.

The temptation to digress from the initial point about the sacredness of Àyànmó would be suspended till later, when I will return, if necessary, to the importance of communal living among these people. Of course, Leku played an important psychosocial and spiritual role in my life trajectory as a younger person; however, the events that introduced her into my life are the pointers to the cultural and supernatural forces that the Yorùbá people are conscious of in their day-to-day lives. It is a common belief among them that coincidence is not an expression of nature and, as such, events in human lives cannot be said to take place by chance or are coincidental. Although humans may not accurately connect the reasons some activities come into play at a particular moment in their lives, this does not undermine the fact that these events are a message by the cosmic originator to align issues and matters in ways to synchronize them with the forces of nature so that everything would be in perfect alignment to make the world continue. I give an example of my exploratory tendency that led me to take a trip to Ilorin as a child. I was fortunate to be around the axis where the train stopped, and seeing that as an opportunity, I decided to follow it to God-knows-where.

My intention obviously was not to travel to Ilorin; after all, I did not have a family with whom I could, by my age and knowledge then, identify or relate to that destination. However, there was a force in me that gave me the energy to embark on the journey. I would tell you how the Yoruba sociocultural milieu makes use of this observation in shaping their cultural and social engagement, by which end it creates the form of society they have had from time immemorial. The people believe that humans are evidence of condensed forces and a body of cosmological power that relays their inherent capacity in different forms. If one is observant, one will notice what dominates or drives individuals from an early stage and how they are exploited to improve their existence. In the Yorùbá environment, there is a cultural practice known as "Akosejaiye," which depicts interpreting the signs and signals of a newborn child to understand the particularities and specialness of the child concerning their subsequent life trajectories. Meanwhile, they know that it is not every member of society who will have the cultural inclination to understand or conduct "Akosejaiye" for their newborn children, and as a replacement, they are very keen on observing the energies that the child exudes as they grow gradually as that would determine how they navigate their existence eventually. This knowledge helps parents to shape who their children become and how their life journeys are structured.

If my parents, and by parents I mean the combination of all the cultural fathers and mothers who constitute the Yoruba household, could not perform my Akosejaiye, they were not ignorant of the understanding that every child carries with them some mystical forces that need interpreting. Mine, apparently, was an exploratory one, and they did not spend much time decoding that in my case and my life journey. I should take a moment to remind you that people's failure to understand their Akosejaiye or perform the alternative, which is the keen observation of the child's dissipated energy, would have consequences on their journey. These values are frozen in their own world, and there is no level of an individual's immersion in other people's cultural traditions that would automatically erase this practice. I can tell you that the relationship between my unsolicited journey to Ilorin, where I became stranded, and my eventual meeting with Leku was just an exercise in the distillation of my cosmic aura. Without one, the other may not be possible, and I will tell you how. By following the train, for example, I gave my parents and maybe guardians the reason to reconsider my life's journey in Ibadan, believing that my exploratory disposition could ruin their parenting on me as they may not be available when I make similar decisions that can truncate my life. Hence, the decision to send me to the rural or an interior setting in Ibadan.

Without the rural environments, I would not have been disposed to the exploratory career through which I have become a known figure today—History. Rural environments are where Yoruba cultural identity is understood in its crudeness and originality. Happiness is shared and people have the opportunity to lean on others to relieve themselves from the burden of life. Others look out for you and ensure that everything in your life is not depressing, and even in cases where the brutal hands of life make you nurse suicidal thoughts, you will still be treated with some admiration to save you from imminent destruction. We were told stories by the elderly ones who served as the custodians and the defendant of the Yorùbá civilization. The stories they told were not externally frozen in time; they depicted present realities and introduced great dimensions to understand life's puzzle. These people would use their cultural brilliance to position their listeners within the context of contemporary happenings, and you will see how today's actions are connected to the events of the past and the role you play in sustaining that. It is evident that you would have a full grasp of life if you had already been baptized in the cultural traditions of the people.

Of course, if it was a coincidence to have traveled to Ilorin on the train without the knowledge of any family member to caution me, would it have also been a coincidence to come back? My return was a result of my efforts in unplanned creativity that made me seek assistance through the popular "almajiri" culture of alms seeking. I say the above to reveal why my being transplanted into an interior part of Ibadan to avoid similar future fearful engagement is an indication that there is an aspect of my life in the future that needed to be discovered in the village. Of course, my parents might not be aware of it, but the energies and cosmic forces I carry were in active work to have enhanced that. Meanwhile, I wanted to be a proper expression of the African world in my very desire to be independent and focused. In the Yorùbá cultural society, people were free and were encouraged to participate in social actions not physically but through the choices they had made in their life trajectory. They are candid believers in the fact that people's decisions and actions always come with consequences. And given this condition, no human action would go without consequences.

To mention the continued importance of Leku to my life will be the most tiring work to do. However, I would make some remarks that showcase them without naming them. In the Yorùbá world, I mean the uncontaminated cultural landscape of the people, individuals are not differentiated based on their gender; instead, they are identified based on their capacity to make fundamental contributions and changes in their environment.

In essence, your power as an individual is not defined by the object between your laps; they are the things that you offer that make the world a fairer place. Although this does not undermine the position of roles in social development, these roles are not gender-sensitive. In the upbringing of the children, everyone is involved, but at a tender age, the woman is more present than the man. This is usually because women are known as the custodians of virtues and values, and their natural proximity to children allows them to inculcate social values into them. The father or man, for example,

comes into the picture when the child is unyielding.
But beyond these two individuals, society is involved in raising them. Just as Leku became very important in the story of my life at that tender age, many other characters too were involved in setting me back to Ibadan from my stray journey to Ilorin.

Moreover, despite the pantheistic disposition of the Yorùbá people to cosmic understanding, they are not fanatics of whatever idea they believe in. Amidst every conviction is the possibility that they may be wrong or that there is no watertight explanation, and then followership, to belief about a specific phenomenon. Having this mental orientation has configured their perspective in such a way that they entertain themselves even when people who are their bloodlines decide to follow different directions in their religion, philosophy, and ideological convictions. Although this democratic culture has brought some unfavorable consequences to the people in some way, it has helped make their cultural identity one of the most dynamic and evolving. Yorùbá people are not the civilization you would be teaching about democracy, especially if by democracy you mean the idea of people condoning others irrespective of their differences. They have a cultural identity attuned essentially to this behavior, which has helped them several times. In spite of Leku's ways of the indigenous culture and engagement, she was not hostile to people who hold different religious views, and this itself has substantially reconfigured my understanding of tolerance and accommodation.

Just like I learned during my stay in the village that human life would always experience changes if it continues on the path of evolution, the experiences I had revealed to me that changes are already imminent in Nigeria's political and historical trajectories. Although the work employs metaphoric expressions to reveal its message, I tell you that it helps to reconnect the lifestyle I spent as a child with the formative years of Nigeria's post-independence years. My childhood period was a time of innocence, confidence, and fairness, and that depicted pre-colonial Africa where the civilizations were loyal to their epistemic infrastructure. They were innocent and would always demonstrate their tender nature without guilt. However, my change of environment to the village can be linked to Nigeria's post-independence, where the unfolding events continue to recalibrate our existence. You would notice that my perception changed, underscored by the mixture of ideas and philosophies that became the sensation of the new environment. That is also something that is connected with Nigeria's post-independence existence. Things became an entirely different experience as people navigate in a more complex political environment that has no respect for their individual creativity and perspective. Although that "growth" became indispensable the moment the African people were visited by the Europeans, it changed their lives nonetheless.

Back to Leku, as you can tell, I seek all the means not to answer questions regarding this figure. Leku herself is an expression of the Yoruba people's expanding world that accommodates people irrespective of their differences. Yorùbá people value sociological relationships, so it is emphasized that anyone who would be acknowledged as a purposeful member of the society would have a strong communal bond with others. While this attribute is a prerequisite for people who want to be seen as an important part of their world, they do not discriminate against those who decide to be different. One such person was Leku, as there was nothing to describe her as an effective sociable and socializing member of the Yoruba society. She was alone in her engagement; she had a restrictive relationship with people within the community. By deliberately avoiding contact with people, everyone knew Leku was an uncommon individual who must be respected and indulged. The indulgence comes from the understanding that despite her secluded lifestyle and reclusive tendencies, she constituted a solid economic force as she specialized in selling materials needed for one or two useful things in their undertakings.

Meanwhile, people did not judge her; she was just seen as an expression of cosmic wonders and unique in her ways. Despite the misconception about her reclusive lifestyle, she indulged me. She became an important part of my childhood experience.

Nothing could be more fascinating than the immense intellectual capacity of Leku, a gift that made her a successful trader of traditional items, especially those related to pharmacology. As a trader in these items, she relied heavily on her sharp memory, which guided her activities when managing her business. Having countless herbs and trees, materials for which people demanded when seeking herbal treatment, Leku would not mistake one item for the other and could accurately describe the place where each item was located, either in her compact room or her shop. What she missed in socializing with others, she made up for it in her photographic memory. I learned first from that being of the limitless capabilities of human neurons to assimilate information as much as possible. The fact that an older woman who is generally expected to have her mind occupied by very different things was demonstrably sound in information keeping and using gave me the motivation to improve myself. I have always opened my arms to positive challenges such as this. I take the challenge, whether from my peers or elderly ones.

In this very case, it was coming from almighty Leku because not only was I miffed by her outstanding efforts in storing information but also I was intrigued by her accurate response to things requested by her customers. Mention what you want to do, and Leku will give you the appropriate herbs.

Sanya Osha: What admirable aspects of Yoruba culture do you think are being lost in the exorable march of modernity and how does this affect you personally and the Yoruba collectively?

Toyin Falola: Answer

The most obvious value I, and I suppose every reasonable Yorùbá person, find admirable is honesty. This is because honesty is the fundamental virtue that determines the activities, nature, and trajectory of people and their civilizations. Without honesty, every other value a person has would not be admired

or consumed by the negativity of lacking honesty.
If one has a remarkable hard work ethic, honesty would determine how far they would go in life. Dishonesty is frowned at among the Yoruba, which was the reason for the relative development that they enjoyed in their primordial environment. Anyone who demonstrates any sign of dishonesty will invite dishonor to themselves, and their innocent relatives will not be spared from the indignity it will bring. To understand the deep-seated connections between the Yorùbá cultural traditions and honesty, one would need to look at their proverbs, axioms, and idiomatic expressions used to emphasize their fixation on an individual's moral character, especially concerning honesty. Such expressions like "bi iro ba lo l'ogun odun, ojo kan soso l'otito a ba" (lies might travel at great speed for many years, but it would be overtaken by the truth within a day).
I would draw a common and practical experience from the Yorùbá world in the olden days. Subsistent farmers who wanted to merchandise their goods were historically said to place them beside the walkways with the attachment of the price tags to the commodities. This culture existed in nearly all the Yorùbá settings. I have some inkling that the culture is still present in some interior parts of the Yoruba world today. People who wanted the commodities procured them and put the price required by the side of the placement or at the spot where the commodity is retrieved. That virtue strengthened the communal bond and system of the people with the understanding that it is worthwhile and dignity-preserving. Economic exchanges happened between the buyer and customer just as you have in big shopping malls today without having to force the people under CCTV or any other similar restrictions. Yet, they maintained a good level of moral conduct that shaped their engagement and empowered them as a people. You should see the difference between the Western system of encouraging honesty and the Yoruba system. You would notice that in the former, people are coerced, while in the latter, the people are convinced. People who do not steal in the shopping malls are, in most cases,

afraid of the security cameras and their consequences, while those who did not steal in the latter were culturally programmed to detest the habit of stealing.

Honesty has been reduced to the barest minimum in contemporary Yoruba society. In fact, mostly in their urban communities, you would be lucky not to be robbed of your belongings at the speed of light when you are in public or private places. The younger generation is unconcerned about what dishonesty will bring them and their family. However, their problems are caused by their older generations who have been consumed by the desire for unmerited benefits, so much so that they are not bothered about how their greed affects the moral compass of others. People want to get rich regardless of the process. They are concerned about increasing their financial networks, not minding the negative impact it would bring if amassed diabolically. They do not bother themselves with what honesty would be for a society losing its communal psychological safety. The philosophy inherent in the saying that "Omo yin o s'agbafo, o nk'aso wa'le, e r'oju ole e o mu" (your child does not have sources of income yet bringing packs of clothes to your house, you defy the urge to arrest a wiling criminal because of your emotional affinity) has lost nearly all its moral credence among the Yorùbá people of modern time. Although the government is complicit in this challenge, it cannot be excused that the people have failed to adhere to their cultural teachings over the urge for personal riches.

Another important value the Yorùbá people place much premium on is hard work. Regardless of your status in the Yorùbá society, the moment you refuse to work for whatever you amass as yours, that is the genesis of your social indignity, which would become everyone's game, including those you believe are below you. Perhaps their understanding of hardworking ethics is woven around the common economic system of their pre-Western civilization. The Yorùbá people were largely agrarian and were very committed to their agricultural engagements. Great people in the community are determined by their ability to coordinate large agricultural activities, as that would determine the extent to which they have economic and financial power. In essence, you must work hard and earn the money you spend. Cutting corners is not celebrated and individuals doing so would always have no place in their communal respect.

People's greatness is directly tied to their capacity to conduct activities that would bring agricultural plenitude and financial buoyance. Yorùbá people brought about the culture of Aaro, which is close in character to what we call thrifting in modern times. In that Aaro practice, a set of people would form a group that would be identified by a name. They would jointly work on members' farmland to cultivate their crops and help in other activities on the individual's farm. That would be rotated until everyone had their farms worked on. To a considerable extent, this practice significantly improved their agricultural production as more men on people far meant more productivity and increased financial stability. This helped to stabilize their economy, and, in the process, people were respected for their ethics in hard work. With time, this culture metamorphosed into thrift-making, which was the economic version of the identified system. What remains very apparent is that people celebrated the virtue of hardworking people, and they developed the younger generation with that cultural orientation. Any individual, especially men, who has come of age and is not disabled, and resisted the responsibility of working hard would be derided and given negative evaluation that would undermine their development in the Yoruba social space. It continued like this because people valued their capacity to contribute to the improvement of society. They believed that when an individual is up and doing, they would reduce the chances of society going into chaos, which assisted in developing the Yoruba world before Western infiltration. Today, not many people are interested in working hard. In fact, many of them are of the understanding that working hard is anti-modernization as they believe working smart pays well. Meanwhile, Yorùbá people who accommodated working hard when the economic mainstay was predominantly agricultural and entrepreneurial would have successfully mutated into working hard with smartness in the modern time. However, the reality is in sharp contrast to what happens in the Yorùbá world today. Quite many of them have incorporated the culture of begging without being concerned about the erosion of their dignity that comes with it. Yorùbá people of the ancient time did not beg. In fact, begging was hated to the extent that beggars were looked down on. However, begging is now glorified in different dimensions in their world today. Able-bodied men and ladies are begging under guises you would never imagine. In the culture of begging, people want things to miraculously change in their world without working for it. I cannot tell you that the religious beliefs that infiltrated the Yoruba world have not perforated their morals in this way. They have reconfigured the minds of the innocent to believe that God would practically do everything they want on their behalf, even when they can make things happen themselves.

Another virtue I value among the Yoruba people is integrated leadership in their sociological makeup. Everyone is a leader by virtue of their membership in that world. You would remember how I was helped by the people in Ilorin to return to Ibadan regardless of their awareness of my inherent exploratory voyage, which, in their estimation, would bring about very strong consequences. They did not need to know my parents, yet they rose to the occasion and ensured I was sent back to my source. And this is where lies the integrated leadership inherent as a value and virtue in every Yoruba person. What mattered to the Yorùbá people was to evaluate if the conditions were right or wrong and would immediately take action if need be. This shows that there is a social system that recognizes what people can do for others regardless of their situation, differences, and their disagreement. Elders generally take up this position as they are considered the pillars of the moral and ideological system of the community. As long as you are a member of that social gathering, they are concerned about your development and would make a substantial effort to intervene in any issue when one is swerving away from the common moral codes of the community.

Everyone respected this arrangement. The manifestations of its effects are found in different dimensions. Social intervention into one's moral indulgence often helps to fix the individual's vision and redirect their steps toward a desirable direction. A child taking what does not belong to them will experience constant admonition from the people, especially the elders. Although they are not giving the child any money in this context, their intervention would help the child understand society's moral obligations and they would desist from actions that are considered outrageous. If the child goes on to become steadfast in what they choose as their career path later in life, they will not undermine the essence of moral values associated with the elders' intervention when they were younger. What was evident was the sincerity of their intentions. They did not admonish people for the sake of downgrading them or making them feel less human. They are merely constructing their moral views to align with the people's conventions. Many times, the parents also admired the practice because they are part of the system that prefers that philosophy. Without withdrawing their efforts, they have ways by which they take responsibility for other children's actions.

People were not accused of persecuting other people's children, nor were there cases of hostile treatment against the people. The culture continued as it has shown a considerable number of positive additions to society. It improved their communal relationships and strengthened their cultural ties. In modern times, I do not think such custom is practiced among them. In fact, it appears that the opposite is the case in the current world. Many children get away with the most horrible things without elders batting their eyelids. This is informed by the regimented hostility that modern parents have against external intervention in their children's negative behavior. Rather than encourage others to intervene when their children are undertaking a morally reprehensible engagement, parents will easily condemn their contributions for flimsy reasons. This has continued to promote all manners of immoral activities among the juvenile. In fact, there are situations where parents are the accessories to the children's immoral engagement. This is usually caused by the parents' dis-education or miseducation about the interrelationship of humans in the inculcation of values into the younger members of the society. Since elders suffer deprecatory comments rather than admiration for their interventions, people unconsciously withdraw from concerning themselves with the issues that deal with others or that relate to something to which they are not attached.

Sanya Osha: Your professional and personal dealings with people are informed by a strong ethic of service. What is the combination of personal and professional elements through which you arrived at this philosophy of life within a community?

Toyin Falola: Answer

To be candid, there are different professional elements or characteristics that enhance relationships with others and strengthen them. These are usually conventional ideas and traits that are necessary and fundamental to fostering a solid interrelationship. Meanwhile, not having them comes with unbearable consequences for individuals. At the personal level, anyone who does not have these qualities in a considerable manner would have difficulty navigating life. These elements are conscientiousness, knowledge, competence, integrity, respect, emotional intelligence, and confidence. Anyone who, for example, does not have knowledge would lack the capacity to drive their life to progress. This is the basic recipe for networking in contemporary times. Knowledge defines a human's ability to get to the crux of events and begin to decipher its most hidden messages, which they use eventually to produce expected results. It is inevitable for many to equip themselves with the knowledge of their environment as the basis for their continued existence. Beyond the knowledge of the environment is the knowledge about a particular profession. While the knowledge of man's surroundings could be useful in the navigation of their personal existence, the knowledge about a profession is needed for advancement in that line. Meanwhile, in a profession, one cannot but deal with others, which again demands another type of knowledge—social interaction.

Knowledge is good for fostering stronger relationships with professional colleagues. Individuals who want to succeed in corporate organizations would have to demonstrate a good level of individual competence. This is necessary because corporate enterprises and bureaucratic institutions usually need competent hands to handle their engagements for outstanding results. You cannot but show your competence unless you are not ready to be sought after in your area of profession. Employers are risk takers, but they do not take risks blindly without taking measures to give them positive feedback. Therefore, they take calculated risks that would bring them anticipated development. A person's service ethics is demonstrated when there is competence because it offers the chance to undertake actions with precision. If you consider the group of people whom I have dealt with or that are still in my professional circle, they are individuals with a great level of competence in their chosen field. With uncommon knowledge, they have channeled their intellectual property to produce resplendent results and are improving their world in their own capacity. Without maintaining that level of outstanding intellection, they would not continue to make waves in their academic and professional environment.

In anything a human is involved in, they must also have a good sense of conscientiousness. This element determines how thorough an individual would be. This is generally necessary to drive an organization forward and make them achieve their potentials.

It is very important that individuals do their work with thoroughness so that they would accomplish their goals. An individual's goal, for instance, would not be accomplished when they refuse to dedicate their mind to it. They need to show that they are indeed ready to accomplish a task before it is possible. This means that their mindset is very important in this thinking.

An individual who is not thorough would handle almost every activity with levity and would care less about the results of their engagements. If they come into a professional or corporate environment with such a mentality, they would, in most cases, not attain the level of success they envisage. This means that while they need to be thorough as individuals, they must also be convincingly thorough in their career or work environment. All the people I have had the privilege of working with have demonstrable thoroughness that has defined our relationship and contributed to our transformation.

It is also a sign of conscientiousness when an individual is careful and vigilant. To be careful at the individual level means one is aware of the intractable complexity that dominates their environment in a way. Therefore, they make calculated efforts to ensure that they do not make errors that would have unbearable consequences. They need to expand this thinking and behavior to their professions. When you consider how well some people handle responsibilities, you will notice that they are of good character and should be worked with. People who are careful in the business environment or workplace would not pay weak attention to issues that would significantly contribute to the advancement of that corporate community. It is as a result of their carefulness that they become vigilant. Being vigilant is an expression of conscientiousness. A vigilant person is conscious of the things that would affect their life and business. Vigilance gives an individual the instinctual capacity to project future challenges and come up with the necessary mechanisms to handle the problems. A careful observation of my circle would reveal how vigilant I am and the people with whom I have worked.

Consequently, having integrity is another value that cannot be negotiated in working with people. This attribute speaks for an individual even when they are not present. A person's integrity can be observed in how they conform to the regulations and instructions of an organization. At the personal level, people's integrity would show in their behavior and adherence to conventional moral standards. These people always value their names and would not compromise their standards, even when induced by external figures. They keep to their ethics and are loyal to the moral principles that they hold in high esteem. They would execute their projects in line with the conventional standards of being a professional while remaining unbroken in the face of challenges. These individuals always attract the respect and confidence of their colleagues because they have proved beyond reasonable doubt that they are considerably disciplined. People with integrity are committed to their actions and are responsible for their deeds. When confronted with overwhelming challenges and temptations that overstretch their integrity, they always demonstrate that their commitment to their principles is far more important than the temptations they encounter at different times. The fact that I surround myself with such people is underscored by my desire to be around the best.

In the same vein, people identify with individuals who show a great level of respect toward others. It is a universal fact that people want to be respected and valued. When people feel disrespected, their possibility to function to the maximum is under probability. This is because being disrespected directly affects one's self-esteem, and when one is low on that energy, one will not function to the maximum. People who are confident in themselves resolve to respect others. People demand respect because it makes them feel good. However, when it is the opposite, they are also somewhat affected in the long run. So, to function effectively, the people we work with need to be accorded their deserved status and respect as that will enable them to give their commitment and maximum contributions. The culture of respect and its expression differ from one group of people to the other. However, in an organization, it is generally important to appreciate people who give their services with a sense of commitment. They would feel better and develop a sense of belonging because their contributions are valued. I would not work with individuals who lack respect, and this philosophy has continued to guide me.

Another important characteristic that people look for in a working environment is emotional intelligence. We do not have to sing it to people that others are going through different challenges that they cannot share with others. Besides, people faced with turbulent challenges would be weighed down when they realize that others did not even showcase their capacity to manage events. Being emotionally intelligent means being aware that others are undergoing stress and challenges in ways that cannot be imagined and not showcasing acts of insensitivity to their plights. One is faced with equal challenges, but it is only through emotional intelligence that one is able to conform to the systems of the organization. The awareness that one is undergoing disruptive issues does not impede an individual from understanding that others may likely be facing a similar experience and that they need to be treated well and with respect. An emotionally intelligent individual does not subvert the feelings of others under the impression that their concerns are not as important as one's indulgence. People would always manage their emotions positively so that work is not disrupted in one way or the other. That person must demonstrate a good level of communication skills and be empathetic.

In the same vein, an individual must be confident in their engagement. Being confident is a recipe for achieving one's goals in life. People must first win in their minds before they can win in real life. Without winning from within, people can find great difficulty achieving their potentials. Confident people always see opportunities ahead of others, and they have the willpower to make moves in these areas. They are not people without the awareness that things and expectations can fail. Instead, they believe that despite the failures of their attempts, they would still make renewed efforts to accomplish their tasks. People with great confidence are an important addition to a group, organization, or enterprise. They exude energy in all their engagements and always walk around with the intention that things will work out for them. They are not empty people. They must have done their due diligence and concluded that there will be light at the end of the tunnel. Their belief in themselves is sometimes contagious. They affect others with their beautiful energies, which comes with a good outcome for an organization.

All these characteristics have affected me positively. I have worked with individuals who are the life of the organization through the confidence that they show in their engagements. Before now, I have dedicated my services to everything I am involved in with a good level of integrity and my life philosophy is already carved from that. I have also improved in my ways of dealing with others, especially regarding how I respect them and their views. Apart from the professional benefit of this behavior, it also allows one to learn from others who share opposite views about life. My emotional intelligence is topnotch because I usually put myself into other people's shoes before I judge their actions. I show a good sense of empathy in my dealings with others, and my confidence level is increased beyond imagination. I am thorough and careful, vigilant and focused in all my engagements, and I have continued to give more doses of these characteristics in whatever I am engaged in. Meeting people and working with them on different platforms have all contributed to my eventual development as an individual.

Sanya Osha: As a historian, what do you consider to be the most fallacious and misleading views held about Africa in general, and what can be done or is being done to debunk them?

Toyin Falola: Answer

There are absolutely many fallacious views that the West specifically and, maybe, the world holds about Africa and, by implication, Africans, which are insulated by the backlog of misinformation they have about the continent and the people. One of them is that Africa does not have history or anything to signal that they have a coordinated past that can fire them into a desirable future. When scientifically observed, this misinform is an instrument for manipulating African people so Europeans would continue to call the short of the continent. I will tell you how this came to be. When the West wanted to embark on their expansionist aspirations that involved the forceful removal of the people from the comfort of their homes to be shipped to another land to exploit them for human labor manifesting in indenture services, the West needed to create a tenable argument that will rid them of a guilty conscience and to justify their nefarious activities. The most effective strategy was to create narratives about their target so that they would have the moral courage to continue with their disingenuous actions. This prompted scientifically unsubstantiated claims such as white people discovering places in Africa; ironically, these places are occupied by different African people.

This narrative of discovering a place where people have otherwise lived for centuries and have their documented history in anthropological legacies appeared to be unsuitable for the enhancement of their agenda as it did not only challenge their barefaced fallacy about discovering the places but also appeared that it was too shambolic to take the people by storm. Eventually, the ones controlling these narratives determined to repackage the entire misinformation to create an opportunity for it to serve them at a different level. That led to the displacement of African history outright. Europeans began to spread the narrative that they were the originator of anything worth mentioning in the African continent and that there was absolutely nothing that could be pinpointed as their past records. The misinformation continued for a long time, apparently because it was effective and served the purpose for which it was created. In faraway Europe and America, the Western sympathizers, that is their reading demographic, therefore, created a wrong image of what Africa and Africans were. That necessitated the unbearable painting of African individuals from that time to the contemporary moment. From the unceasing peddling of misinformation to the people, one of the underlying issues was that people in the communities mentioned above imagined that Africa wasn't a country.

But that would not stop there, as this became more effective in the social and political world than in other areas of human life. Gradually but steadily, they redirected the narrative to the academic environment as they deliberately doctored information and distorted history so that they would continue their quest to cover their negative deeds. Such unsubstantiated claims were immediately raised, such as stories like Africa(ns) never had political, social, economic, scientific, technological, religious, and even philosophical history. Although all these would eventually become very potent in their desire to dislodge the historical legacies of the people, what was more infuriating was that the West was actively investing in the re-engineering of the minds of the people, both Africans and the willing global audience, against the understanding that it would help them create a solid foundation for their mischief and disingenuous engagements. They began with the use of religion, and their conclusion was that African spirituality was shambolic and pagan and would never have a place in the construction of a modern environment. They began by using it as their point of harsh campaign against the Black people. To say a people do not have religious and spiritual existence is the most crushing attack that could be launched against Africa.

You would notice that everything became interconnected eventually, and I would unpack their unity. In the religious blackmail, the African people were poised to accept an alternative religious model to have the legitimacy of spiritual essence to see themselves as part of the evolving society. Meanwhile, the alternative religious identities offered by the West were also an instrument of control that would facilitate the acceleration of their expansionism through the recalibration of their minds and the reclusion of their indigenous spirituality. The problem was going to be more magnificent than the people could potentially handle. It was also the plan work of the West to consolidate their mind reprogramming with their ideological convictions, which are perforated enough to carry their sentiment across to the African minds in the percentage needed for their colonialism advancement. Africans were exposed to Western education and isolated the minds of the people from the indigenous values that might have been their guidance against an external ideological worldview that contradicts their epistemic legacies. The African mind in Western schools became a potent instrument in repudiating the African indigenous ontological ideas.

Consequently, they became an active participant in dismantling African values, especially the religious ones. Under the impression that they wanted to win accolades from their masters, a lot of this new generation of Africans participated actively and effectively in the disorientation of the African religious relics. The successful capture of their minds began to yield positive results for the Western world in different dimensions, so much so that even at the termination of the colonial relationship, they became willing collaborators in the final excoriation of the African religious fabrics. Whereas all that was needed for the smooth control of the people's minds was that they have minds captured already, every other thing would definitely make way for itself. The fact that there were sufficient academic materials unapologetically saying that Africans did not have history indicates that the West has succeeded in their plans against the people. I would give a very shining example of this. Before the ascension of the West into the African countries, trade relationships existed that transcended cultural boundaries and penetrated political landscapes. People conducted businesses together and exchanged values, including the trade routes between Africa and the East.

Suddenly, in post-independence Africa, when there was a developed modernization and globalization of unknown magnitude, Africans found it difficult to conduct trade relationships among themselves. As a historian, it would be noticed that the situation I have painted tilts toward the already generated assumption and misconception that the African people never had history. You would ask yourself a very simple question at that level: if truly the African people of the past had history, was there no trade or economic history in it? This suggests that as the West is making claims, unsubstantiated as they were, they are also making political efforts to ensure that the claims are valid. An average African would sneer that off and water it down as though it was unnecessary, but the West understood very well how committed it was to destroying the African fabric. They have divided the continent in line with their ambitions and would create imaginary boundaries that would enhance their ambition. In essence, the Francophone African person thinks of their association and loyalty to the French first before they would even consider their closest neighbors, who had the British as their colonial lords. The Anglophone Africans would first see themselves from the prism of the West in terms of European culture and ideas before they see themselves as one with the proximal African.

The implication is that there has been a successful diasporization of the African continent, which enables the people within the continent to be far from one another even when they are literally occupying the same space. In essence, the Africans in Nigeria would prefer refining their crude oil even when he has the financial power to construct refineries. Although this would not be a problem when we consider the greater damage that is done through the actions and inactions of others. While the Nigerian government would do this, there was no strong institution that would rise from other African countries and make them see the negative effects of their actions. Countries would become accomplices in the degeneration of African land through terror and chaos when they decide to become reticent to issues that concern their safety and security, but as long as they are not directly affected, they are comfortable with that arrangement. All these are the various ways the African people of the contemporary world are helping the West to prove their misconception right through their actions. That explains why an Uncle Sam would invade Libya to silence one of the leading Africans doing well economically, and the *unity* in the OAU would become watery.

In one of the recent interviews granted by Wole Soyinka, he lamented how the lack of history, meaning information, was the foundation of the Nigerian problem. I would expand his argument by saying that the fundamental problems of Africa and Africans began from the permission they granted to unscientific claims that they come from the West. In essence, the solution would begin with undoing what they have done. This is why many scholars are concerned about decolonization. Decolonization is a process of self-rediscovery, a process of reflection and a process of purification. Of course, some serious contenders and critics argue that the invulnerability of the West does not come from Africa's refusal to embrace their own historical past, as put forward by the decolonialists, but from their inability to use their current time very effectively. Whereas their argument is reasonable and tenable, its pursuance does not promise to give us the anticipated development. For example, Chinua Achebe and Wole Soyinka, among other African scholars, apart from agitating for the domestication of Western ideas, have done well in their liter trade, yet there has been no positive sign that Africans have a unique identity in the world.

When an individual is forced to drink poison that can numb their system, it would be counter-productive to advise them to continue to use vitamins or supplements with the idea that such would renew their strength and give them more life. The fact is that even when their body system is renewed through these supplements, it would only prepare the system ready for a different feast by the inbound poison. The supplements may offer momentary solutions, but they would never bring general wellness. What the decolonization advocates are doing is that the said poison should be gradually drained away from the body system, although this would be done very carefully, gradually, and will be piecemeal. By steadily drilling out the colonial poison, the African people would heal gradually until they find their way to their identity, as that would help them create a strong civilization that they could defend with their own ideas. People in the modern day confuse large and great infrastructure with civilization while, in the real sense, these things are the outward results of the people's civilizational philosophy. If it is not your philosophy and you build skyscrapers, maintaining it will be difficult and, at a point in time, you would run into greater challenges.

Sanya Osha: In your earlier work, you focus on the scholarly contributions of Yoruba intellectuals such as Odunjo, Samuel Johnson, and a host of others. How do you think these various colonial-era thinkers navigated the tradition/modernity divide and what can we learn from them?

Toyin Falola: Answer

We would understand the magnitude of the intellectual engagements that these pioneer scholars of Yorùbá origin did when we begin to understand that what we can draw from their intellectual property is inexhaustible. J. F. Odunjo and Samuel Johnson are two Yorùbá writers whose works became disruptive to the established Eurocentric narratives that reconfigured the African identity and became an important reference point for the scholars coming after them. It should be emphasized that the idea of raising your voice through pen requires many things. In fact, it is a very risky adventure that people go into. Apart from the fact that you would have to struggle for readership and draw the base of competitors' audience, you would require a reasonable amount of money to continue in that trajectory. Writing is such an arduous task that it almost gives results that are not commensurate with the efforts, especially in the past. Taking the frontal role in the brave engagements means that these scholars we have mentioned have laid a very solid foundation for promoting African values, even if it comes at their personal cost. Many African countries were vulnerable and helpless to the scheming of the West because not only did they not have their audience from the continent, but they also would have to convince the global readership community of their intellectual differences.

In the case of Samuel Johnson, for example, many conditions made his works greater and more powerful in the writing industry. One of such conditions is the appropriation of the colonial language as an instrument of message transmission to the audience. It should be noted that while it was the ambition of the scholars of this period to wrestle their identity from the claws of the West as it was almost impossible to gather themselves appropriately for reasons that are not very distant from the efforts already put in place by the same Western imperial order. For example, the application of the English language to offer their ideas is a way to protest the various misinformation handed down against the African people and, by implication, a way of negotiating the audience from the same West. Apparently, their writing was meant to correct the wrong impression and notions against them, but how that would be accepted by Eurocentric readers was an issue to consider. Regardless of the apparent hurdles that they needed to cross, they continued with their work and sent the necessary protest to the Western community about their unwillingness to continue in their slavery entrapment. They resisted and protested the Europeans' domination of their cultural and epistemic space.

In essence, Samuel Johnson's work became an important instrument in resisting Eurocentric misconceptions and to fight against their ambition to keep them perpetually in the dustbin of history. The more the African people acquired Western education and knowledge, the more they had access to Johnson's works, which began to open their eyes to the myriad of African values that have been hitherto condemned, relegated or undermined. From his works, they knew that there were important monuments of history that were Yorùbá-bound, and this opened their eyes to the dimensions of issues which, like the Yorùbá history, the West had deliberately given a negative outlook. In addition, we continued to benefit more specifically from interdisciplinary and transdisciplinary ideas that would be used to advance various fields of academic engagements in contemporary times. More than it would have been predicted, the writings of these scholars have garnered more attention and interest that propelled subsequent scholars into digging more about their historical legacies. They became outliers in their engagement because their contributions have continued to propel the people into acting and scheming against the eternal domination of the West.

From Johnson's works, budding scholars of the African intellectual divide could get information about the anthropological legacies of the Yoruba people. Beyond this, they used the works of the time as the instrument of history that revealed to them the unending resources of the people with regard to past events. Also, those pursuing language knowledge could have more specific information about the Yoruba language and linguistic science. Their works literally became the Bible that the new sets of intellectual Yorùbá people and scholars were using. Whether the aspect of knowledge received more academic attention or not was subject to the encouragement and findings that people in that line of discipline were interested in making. Most of their works became pioneer intellectual materials that are referenced even today. The fact of originality cannot be rubbed off of their works as they involved thorough intellectual exercises that offered detailed information about whatever they have chosen to write about. The people's social life was also known through the materials produced by some of these scholars and more during the highlighted period. It was the combination of efforts of the generation in question that produced a lexicographic legacy for the Yorùbá people.

J. F. Odunjo also showed his prolific capacity in the works he wrote in the Yorùbá language. To function within their timeline in that capacity depicted them as brilliant and extremely endowed with strong or formidable willpower. Writing in Yorùbá was a complete gamble during the time in question. For one, its readership is not generally expected to move beyond the geography of the Yorùbá world, where people primarily used the language. This means that apart from the potential limitations of economic growth that would attract the writer, there was also the risk of not being heard behind the cultural boundaries of the identity.

In reality, this was more like committing intellectual suicide. Considering the complex processes of book publications and the financial demands of the possible investment, anyone who did not make concessions with debt and penury would consider it very carefully before taking the risk. But the urge to make an impact appealed more to the minds of the people than they urged for economic gains, and they converted their energies into making or investing in scholarships that project their cultural identity to the world. This explains why the field of Yorùbá education today has some prominent researchers who have done exceptionally well to advance the world and knowledge of the people.

If you asked me how they navigated between tradition and modernity, I would reveal to you that their focus was on transformational and developmental ideas and ideals beyond the rhetoric of personal aggrandizement that has dominated the world today. Even when they got an educational experience colored by Western epistemology, they did not allow that to upend their indigenous values. There was still a time when virtue was celebrated collectively and people placed much importance on an individual's character. With his Alawiye book series, Odunjo became an important force in the transmission of the Yorùbá knowledge and ideas to the people of the younger generation. His works stood tall and continued to expand the frontiers of academic resources, moral principles, ideological convictions, and epistemic configuration of Yorùbá people handed down in good language and driven into the readers' subconscious. Children of the period did not waste much of their time before they knew the general moral ideals of the Yorùbá and were genuinely happy to identify with that cultural tradition and identity for decades.

On this note, there are innumerable things we can learn from them. Apart from the fact that writers are meant to serve as the conscience of the people, we also understood from them that many things are generally possible when a scholar dedicates their attention to certain goals. Samuel Johnson remained the conscience of the people, especially because converting the language of Yoruba into English was a tedious engagement. Of course, his works are part of the pioneer materials that one can lay hands on during the period in question. Now you can begin to imagine what people like that went through in the process of documentation. They became strong and wanted to channel their intellectual energy into something profitable for a whole race. More than this, their works became the available source of information for the coming generation and an important reference to counter the wrong assumptions of the West and invalidate several unsubstantiated conclusions that are in circulation against the said people. The implication was that they gave people the necessary confidence to embark on the intellectual journey of self-discovery. If their works had not been in existence, the West would have further stretched their negative scheming against the African people.

Odunjo became an important force in the world of decolonization. For one, the fact that someone in that period could document the African experience in their mother tongue and would receive widespread acceptability planted the advocacy for freedom in many people. Everywhere in the world, the culture of protest is considered very important in the political process of people. In this case, a protest was staged using the intellectual properties of the pioneers, and their works became an effective tool to repudiate the malicious intentions of the West. Simultaneously, their works woke the sleeping giant in any African people to come to its full potential. They have breathed life into what a number of us are doing today. We can pick the works of these individuals and begin to explore very different layers of academic works that would add important value to issues raised in contemporary times. It would be noticed that global-wide outreach of Yoruba scholarship today would not be possible without the efforts put in place by outstanding individuals.

Sanya Osha: You also worked extensively in conjunction with other researchers on ancient Yoruba cosmology and spirituality. Why has this been central to your work and why did you make it your concern to see that these often-suppressed worldviews are accorded their rightful status within Yoruba society and other related ones?

Toyin Falola: Answer

Without negating the understanding that human consciousness is directly tied to their compliance to the cosmological awareness interpreted by a certain community of people, conversations with nature too have always occurred at the level of cultural interactions and inclinations of the people. This means that one's positional advantage in getting a better understanding and then relationship with nature would have to be determined by the point where the individual is in relation to the cosmological understanding of their group identity. In essence, the possibility or tendency for impactful existence is determined by how much the individual understands the proper way of navigating the world that is full of energies that the cosmic community has put in place. Although the programs of nature are designed by the originator, of course, this might appear complicated for individuals already caught up in the world that believes everything in the universe is self-generated, but that does not underplay the reality that the world has a fixed language with which it communicates to people and phenomena. If one does not understand the cosmic designs through the prism of one's ontological composition, one will live the experience of others with whom one identifies with their cosmic beliefs. It is a basic truth that cannot be dislodged so easily.

The fact that you do belong to a particular religious or spiritual community of groups of people other than your own or do not subscribe to spiritual beliefs at all does not mean you are off the hook of all cosmological calculations. Instead, it means the position you hold is an expression of other people's understanding of the universe, by which case you are also demonstrably cosmic-conscious only in the pattern of such group's understanding. Meanwhile, one's alignment with one's indigenous epistemic and ontological foundations naturally helps in many ways to understand who one truly is in the scheme of things. This is generally informed by the awareness that people's interpretation of cosmic forces and programming determines to a large extent how they interpret humanity, what being human means, and by implication, how one views oneself in the grand scheme of things. In essence, a Christian who, by Christological cosmic awareness, conceives the world as a place dominated and exclusively run by the cosmic power from which they establish a distance would also develop values and moral virtues that are in synchronization with such orientation. Let me try to explain this. Religious individuals who, for example, cry and feel remorse when praying are possibly operating from the understanding of the universe that their cosmic construction has offered them has to be committedly pacified before their whims and caprices can be indulged. This is so because they conceive the universe as something they are isolated from and would therefore need to be sober in getting the things they need from nature.

Consequently, that thinking develops a social philosophy that conditions people to be sober when they want to get anything from others. Meanwhile, being sober is a good moral principle that would be appreciated in the world around. However, the underlying shortcomings are inherent in the idea that the individual would see themselves as borderline powerless and would depend only on fate. Professor Wole Soyinka disclosed in one of his granted interviews of which title I cannot specifically remember, that the "doctrine of resignation was not acceptable in the (cosmological understanding of) Yoruba worldview." This implies that the construction of human behavior is not distant from their perception of the universe itself. It is in the awareness that man takes a particular position in relation to the universe that they shape the form of moral, ideological and ethical principles that define them. As a further explanation, there are quite a number of civilizations that place a premium on karma, for example. The understanding that the activities and actions of a people constitute a cyclone of force that they have generated, which would therefore have its accompanying reaction, dwells in the conviction that nature is organized and maybe programmed in a particular way. In one way or the other, all these things are expressions of cosmic understanding and knowledge.

Having provided this foundation, I would want to explore some of the cosmological interpretations identified by the Yorùbá people from where I come, but I would do so with respect to some important analogies. Have you ever seen individuals who, despite the mountain of challenges and tribulations they are confronted by in life, and all their engagements, would always come up unscathed and undefeated as though they faced nothing? Have you, at the same time too, heard people allude to their very strong cosmic presence, which manifests in different expressions of human languages, such as in Yorùbá saying that "Orí e le" (he has a strong or undefeatable head, where the head means destiny)? This expression finds similar socio-religious comments made in the Christian world when they say someone oozes grace from above. This, right here, is a shining indication of the respective world's understanding of the cosmic arrangements and their composition. But since we are discussing the cosmic forces as interpreted by the Yorùbá people, it is necessary that we dive into some of these things. Yorùbá people, for example, believe in Orí, Àyànmó, and the indestructibility of the metaphysical world where the actions and activities of man are generally programmed. This has informed the deep-seated connections between them and the unseen forces and, in reality, has, in a way, helped in the redefinition of their roles in this arrangement.

Orí and Àyànmó are a part of the cosmo-spiritual configuration of the universe that Yorùbá people have made a keen observation and then evaluated so that they would continue to lead their lives in a particular direction. Orí is considered the soft head of the human realization, which represents the human when there is no consciousness. This means that the human consciousness and their Orí are phenomena that work in complimentary circles, but one definitely precedes the other and therefore is meant to be more powerful. The literal interpretation of Orí is head but its cultural understanding has a more nuanced appreciation. Human consciousness comes when they are alive and grows with their time on Earth, but their Orí preceded them because it began from man's initial condition in the metaphysical world. I would take you to our knowledge of biology, where the reptile-like shape of the human sperm was explained to us as the foundation of human existence. The Yorùbá interpretation of this is closely linked to such meaning. But what is very enthusing or maybe surprising generally was that the contemporary understanding of human sperm as having that structure is informed by the use of vision aid (binoculars, microscope, among others). What I am trying to say here is that at the beginning was Orí whose journey started in a place where we have no consciousness.

Meanwhile, the Yorùbá people believe that it was the said Orí that made a series of decisions during man's initial condition, at which time man had no consciousness. Apparently, consciousness builds man's conscience. Assuredly, when Orí made the various choices in that domain of existence, it now remains the role of Eledumare, who is regarded as the central cosmic originator, to grant each of the things that Orí has selected. Now, this is where it gets very interesting. Eledumare is aware of the various choices that others have made and knows what situations, circumstances, and conditions would aid the actualization of man's metaphysical desires, and for this reason, Eledumare would place humans within the necessary environment where their chosen ambition would be actualized. In essence, one would wonder why some people would be born into a wealthy family while others are sent to poor ones, especially when neither of them has the opportunity of choosing this reality. In essence, the individuals will begin to navigate their existence in line with what they have chosen and were programmed to get in their consciousness state when living on Earth. People who face tribulations would complain, and the ones that are placed in better conditions would celebrate, neither of them knowing why they are towing the very path on which they found themselves.

I have only given you a snippet of the cosmological understanding of Yoruba especially concerning human and supernatural existence. In essence, all of these have been central to my work and even worldview, apparently for different reasons. Like I have conceded elsewhere that scholars are the conscience of their people and the frontliners of their collective ideas, it is a moral burden that we take action to salvage things that are getting less attention even when we understand that they have importance in our engagement. The spirituality of the Yorùbá people is keenly associated with their social development and accounts for the reason why their cosmological worldview should not be undermined. Through a number of years of unalloyed loyalty to their cosmological interpretation, they have instituted behavior, ideologies and character that deserve preservation. But since these things are not frontally known and advocated, it has continued to erode the values of the people in ways that cannot be prevented except when very important and bold steps are made. To take as an example, children who are born into a certain household in the contemporary Yorùbá world do not understand the socio-spiritual connections that they have as a people, and that has dwindled their values considerably.

It is therefore a matter of personal ambition to make efforts so that all these would be corrected and necessary steps taken for the restoration of the effaced values. An individual who does not understand the underlying spiritual essence of their family, for instance, would be doomed to undertake activities that potentially would drive them away from what is necessary. Take, for example, an individual who is not aware that their family has a track record of being morally upright and might get drawn into engagements that soil their name and, by implication, erode their spiritual essence. I have chosen to take up this great responsibility over the awareness that an age-long misconception about the

African ontological and epistemological perception has contributed to the sterilization of their cultural values, even in ways that are too obvious to be disregarded. As a scholar, I believe I owe society the responsibility to beam the torchlight of research into this area so that we would have a collective reawakening.

Although there are some available texts that have offered an interesting perspective on the issues of African spirituality, my angle of research has helped to promote what the Yorùbá people have as their spiritual worldview, and my works have made efforts to place them within the appropriate context of cosmological views of Africans generally. If we need any inspiration to continue in that trajectory, the impressive milestones that the Yorùbá spirituality is making in the global community are enough for involvement in any such activity, so we would complement their contributions through what we are doing in scholarship. There is an inseparable connection between people's spirituality and the position they are in in the cosmic arrangements. Our physical existence is a continuation of a world that is already perfected in some ways. The more we associate ourselves with the interpretation given to these things by our sociological identity, the more we understand our roles as individuals and also a participant in the entire process. We cannot underestimate the magnitude of mental freedom that one is capable of achieving when one makes an eternal resolution with their indigenous ontological views, as that would open them to the actual freedom that they need to navigate the world excellently.

Sanya Osha: Can you discuss the aspects of ancient and modern African intellectual culture that have made the most noteworthy contributions to world culture at large?

Toyin Falola: Answer

Generally, intellectual culture has been argued to aim at clarifying people's thinking about the urban and the rural environment through the agency of discourse-led research in the cultural context of the world of a people, including their architecture, medical science, aesthetics, science, technology, and theories among other things. If we concede to this definition, it is therefore not unexpected that we would be in synchrony with the realization that the development of knowledge epistemologies in Africa has been something related to their intellectual culture. Although many scholars of colonial and postcolonial times have dipped their hands into the epistemic resources of the West from which their knowledge is handed down, that does not automatically make them distant from the intellectual history of their people. Apart from the committed Western apologists and their intellectual writings, there is a group of African writers whose works have been generally inspired by African intellectual history. This community, where I belong, has always relied on the inexhaustible intellectual resources of the African past as the foundation of our intellectual engagement in contemporary times. This cannot be helped when it is realized that apart from the extraordinary excellence of the said resources and their quality, they are also very instructive in creating a worthwhile environment.

One of the apparent African intellectual cultures that has continued to make itself relevant in current times is the African perception of gender relationships in community building. But to understand the African fair gender ideas, one has to contrast them with what is obtained in the Western world. Europeans had a culture that considerably relegated the women folks in their patriarchal endorsement, and that was enhanced by a collective history which necessitated that behavior. That history is relished in wars and hostilities, among other things, and they developed a culture out of that sense of protection against their women. However, there are other sides to this. There is an angle that believes that women were outright taken away from the political and economic processes by which condition they become impotent in the matters that concern the social welfare of the community. What is important to us in this context is that the same European came with that ideological consciousness to dominate Africa where their cultural behavior did not permit such division or relegation. More than any other thing, many African civilizations considered women as the natural custodians of their culture over the understanding that they occupy an integral position in the arrangement of the world. Through political power during colonialism, women were pushed far from politics, and this created a stigma. Meanwhile, the growing African politicians were studying the patterns and unconsciously assimilating the values of the West. By the time they grabbed power to the fullest, they had begun to replicate the idea and customs of the Europeans, which they had inculcated while they were relegated to the background. Although some would argue that the eventual dismembering of the women folks by post-independence African politicians was motivated by two important reasons; one, the urge to displace every memory or legacy of the West so that they would continue on a better pedestal, and two; the outright likeness to retain power and be worshipped by the people who do not have it. In the case of women, politics saw them as the necessary collateral to continue in their insensitive pursuit of gender discrimination in the corridor of power. Whatever the reason, the African history of gender parity was effaced gradually but effectively. They became concerned more with power than they were interested in the fair distribution of power in their society. Meanwhile, African women were not going to embrace this new role forced on them by the neocolonial populations that were determined to push into the background anything that potentially challenged them. Protests such as the popular one from Olumilayo Ransom Kuti, the mother of the erstwhile Afrobeat music, Fela Anikulapo-Kuti, were instances of the violent disagreement of the available order against the supremacist ambition.

Seeing what the system introduced, especially in that gender world, was uncelebrated by the African people, intellectuals began to draw from the legacy of African intellectual culture to bring out many instances of gender relationships as conceived and operated by the pre-colonial African people. This was necessary for their determination to realign their society with the right forms of values that are drawn from their indigenous backgrounds and systems. When you consider the Yorùbá cultural world, for example, you would notice that in spite of their patriarchal consideration, it was generally vibrant and fair when it came to their gender relativity. For instance, apart from the kingship stool that they reserve for men, ministerial positions occupied by chieftaincy titles are distributed according to the sensitivity to gender existence in the community. To that extent, while men would be given the ministerial position of security and safety, apparently because of their disposition to that role, the woman would be accorded the role of maintaining the economy. In essence, every important role in the community is shared with a good level of fairness to gender identity. If the West has therefore come to disrupt this arrangement momentarily, that does not give the neocolonialists the freedom or the moral victory to continue with extensive gender inequity in post-independence.

Another important African intellectual culture that we have continued to explore is its aesthetics. It remains an anthropological reality that aesthetics developed essentially from the African continent and that most of the globally celebrated icons whose works of art are appreciated across civilizations and age drew their inspirations from African aesthetics. In fact, this appears like one of the most obvious items that continue to speak loud legacies of the people from their time. All across the world, especially in renowned museums in the world, there is a large deposit of African art from different countries and cultures in modern times. Most of these artifacts are kept in the heart of the colonizers' museums in Europe and also in America. The fact that they have continued to attract tourists and audiences is an indication that they are a distinct product that showcases raw talent and astute ingenuity. The question that should come to your mind here is, if the artistic productions of the past 400 or 500 years are still marveled at and also sought after in the contemporary time, that is evidence that they are made from the staple of refined knowledge deposited in a people who have uncommon desires for exploring their innate ingenuity. Although some African countries participated in this more than their colleagues elsewhere, what you would not find in scarcity is the aesthetics of the people.

In essence, all these have been transformed in our contemporary intellectual discourses and activities. Considering that the pre-colonial Africans valued aesthetic engagements, like singing, sculpture making, etc., all these have been transformed into magnificent activities in modern times. You go to America, and you realize that the likes of Ayo Balogun, who is popularly referred to as Wizkid, and Damini Ogulu, popularly called Burna Boy, are dominating the musical world there in spite of coming from thousands of kilometers away. You go to South America, and you come across the beautiful artistic productions of Africans dominating their market, and also go to Europe, you find that there is a large deposit of African aesthetics, and you would realize that the African intellectual culture has not only metamorphosed, it has also taken the space unabated. It would therefore reveal to you that the direction of the African scholarship in this intellectual property is an indication that they are consciously employing their intellectual heritages to expand their academic and professional engagement in the contemporary time. One beautiful development of African intellectual culture is the fact that Africans in all countries of the world have fought for the incorporation of African Studies in their various university institution, and this has opened several opportunities for the integration of African knowledge systems into these places.

The birth of that institute in various universities in the world, including the ones in the continent, has seen the introduction of knowledge engagements that seek to provide answers to issues from the perspectives of Africans. This has led to the initiation of programs and disciplines that are made for the facilitation of African knowledge in chosen fields. Consider, for example, that one of the said departments in African Studies is the African trado-medical area of knowledge that is integrated. It is possible within this discipline to continue to probe medical research from the viewpoint of

Africans. This means that all the historical activities that are fossilized, the engagement of the past are gradually excavated for re-examination and interrogation so that people would see if there are ways by which African medical knowledge can help provide solutions to contemporary challenges.

This has led to substantial educational engagements of the people in the said institute across places where they are in the world. By probing available anthropological evidence, these individuals have been able to uncover massive information about medicine as practiced by people in the time past. The focus of academic engagements has therefore been one which seeks to establish the validity of the African medical awareness in relation to its potential to change the global order of medicine application. It has therefore been discovered in the process that the medical system of the West, to a considerable extent, consolidates their individualism philosophy which, among other things, seeks to disconnect with anything that is considered an impediment. Unlike the Western medical system, however, the African one gives a different approach.

In Africa, for anyone suffering from any form of ailment, they always make it possible to use corrective solutions with minimum side effects. Rather than relying on preserved drugs, the African people used available medical resources to solve their problems. Of course, one will possibly argue that with the advancement of contemporary medical experiences, how would such a practice be effective in this context? The right response to such questions would be that these people addressed all manners of challenges they had then; they can still use that system today.

Since this has been refined in the contemporary academic engagements, it would be noticed too in the process that Africans have been coming up with different theoretical arguments and conversations across various disciplines in the contemporary. Most of these scholars draw from the resources of their African past, where they dug materials that are employed for the crystallization of their academic values. These theories are used to interact with the phenomenon of lives that are raised in many areas of knowledge. In the field of literature, for example, there are numerous theories that are proposed in African scholarship, which, among other things, are meant to help in the interpretation of the African literary writings, and these theories too have proved to be of international value as well. There are many scholars of African literature who have contributed to this feat. We can say the same thing with philosophy as an academic discipline. In fact, quite a number of African philosophers have proposed various theories that introduce the philosophical convictions of the people as opposed to the ones to which they have eternally been glued through Western education. All these continue to prove that they have a resourceful history from where they always draw for their intellectual development. Scholars in History have also done similar laudable things in African intellectual culture.

In addition, one of the greatest aspects of ancient and modern African intellectual culture is the Yorùba Orisa. It is not surprising, therefore, that the Yorùbá Orisa is making a substantial spread by breaking a different level of records overseas wherever it is introduced. Yorùbá Orisa traditions venerate the outstanding characteristics of a particular deity whose attributes and characteristics are adapted by their followers. These Orisa are believed to have demonstrated supernatural attributes in their lifetime as they undertook extraordinary services that brought to the advancement of societies. There hardly was any area of life that the people did not have outstanding characters as deities in the primordial Yorùbá cultural world. Those deities are usually the connecting links between peoples and the extraterrestrial forces and use that capacity to expand the frontiers of Yorùbá in many different ways. Their pioneer efforts yielded numerous results for the Yorùbá and the people adopting them in a different environment. This is why many other civilizations mostly embrace them in contemporary times. It was, for instance, the beyond-human attributes of Ogun that led to the inspiration of the people to make technological progress.

These people, for instance, experienced transformation in different areas of life in accordance with the attributes of their Orisa.

Gods such as Ogun, Sango, Aje, Osayin, and goddesses such as Osun, Oya, and Iyemoja all made outstanding achievements in their various departments, and they, therefore, were adopted exalted positions in the cosmological system of the people. Osun, believed to be the goddess of beauty and productivity, was embraced in Latin America, particularly Brazil, because of the socio-spiritual roles that she played in their cultural and religious evolution. They have, therefore, integrated Osun as part of their Orisa worship over the belief that they would continue to be protected, loved, and appreciated by the same power. It goes without saying, for example, the roles it played during the period of slavery when many Africans were subjected to harsh and hostile treatment by the enslavers. Aje was considered the Orisa in charge of wealth creation and distribution, and for this reason, she should be propitiated and celebrated so that the individual would benefit greatly from her. There was the Osayin, known to have the intellectual capacity to understand the various uses of herbs and trees. That was central to the sustenance of humans, and the fact that it became a celebrated engagement strengthened its place among them.

Apart from the Yorùbá Orisa, which is a part of the African intellectual culture that is doing exceptionally fine in the world, there also is the philosophy of Ubuntu that is making impressive waves in the world today. Ubuntu is that African philosophy that emphasizes collaborative and integrative existence. The philosophy underpins the importance of living to enhance other people's happiness as different from the person's provincial values. It is summed up in the saying, "I am because we are, and since we are, therefore I am." This philosophical expression argues that the valuation of human lives lies in the ability to be interdependent. This is necessary because they discover that an individual cannot be self-righteous, nor can they be self-sufficient. To that extent, they news others in their lives so that they can lead positive and influential lives. If they did not subscribe to each idea, it would be realized that they are potentially exposed to challenges capable of consuming them. By making it a social philosophy, they have therefore mandated everyone to make conscious efforts to contribute toward the development of others as that would invariably determine how far they would go. This helped them in creating the social structure that they have.

In contemporary times, Ubuntu as a social philosophy seems to have traveled far beyond the shores of the African continent. This is underscored by the fact that those Africans who found themselves in the Global North or other places in the world either by the event of slavery or those that found their ways to the diaspora through movement have continued to live that philosophy because more than it might have been imagined, they have continued to unite themselves or organize their events together as a formidable group. They did not limit their moral principles entrenched in the philosophy to their African members alone; they extended that orientation to others in different engagements where they found themselves. This has therefore helped in uniquely identifying Africans in all their doings. When they continue with that mindset, they will attain better heights where other aspects of their existence would have been reasonably expanded. There cannot be a contention that it would intensify the efforts of the powerful Africans whose offices statutorily determine how far the people would go. We should be reminded that all these happen because various Africans are making all manners of contributions to their different areas.

Sanya Osha: Why do you think Africa and her peoples have been vilified, violated, and dehumanized over the course of history and why does this state of affairs persist till today?

Toyin Falola: Answer

Let me begin by invoking a popular axiom in Africa that people do not tamper with a barren tree. This saying is developed from the awareness that humans are naturally attracted to productive trees which bear fruits. Since a barren tree does not produce fruits, however, it becomes understandable why they argue that individuals would not tamper with it because they are unattracted to it. The beginning of Africa's and Africans' vilification was the discovery of human power, which the continent possesses, and this history is a recent one—about 500 years ago. The Arabs, in their trade engagements with Africans, spread the message of African greatness to the world, who received it with awe. Biologically, the African human is built to possess a mass of energy that can be used for different purposes. They understood that this attribute is useful in the expansion of agricultural engagements as there will be enough human capital to successfully organize and manage the agrarian system, an engagement that the West was irrevocably committed to. As such, the first journey of the Europeans to Africa emerges with the understanding that the former wanted to explore the continent to view from a close range the magnificent human resources that have been disclosed in their world. If it was true that Africa has strong biology, it was logical that the Western world devise the means by which they could capture it.

At this juncture, vilification comes in as an instrument of achieving their potential. Africa and Africa must be vilified for the West to achieve their imperialist ambition, and it seemed there were two ways to enhance that; missionary and slavery. Missionary work was the liberal instrument that was to be used as their initial weapon. If it failed, there would be another. And even if it did not, certainly, there would be other methods introduced. The hard truth is that the missionary is the imperialist wing that was given the responsibility of destroying the African man from a spiritual angle. By first installing in their mind the sentiment that their spirituality is weak and not capable of fighting for them, they prepared the minds of the African people for the layers of vilification, slander, and malicious intentions that they would embark on eventually. Africans who were not tied exclusively to their religious beliefs had the freedom to embrace the new faith, and they continued to be re-engineered to loathe their ontological understanding in exchange for the West's views. Do not forget that the place these Europeans were going was the retrieval of the African human resources for their own provincial advantages. Meanwhile, once the African man was conquered in their minds, they either became willing instruments of further destruction or volunteered to drive people for the European agenda.

In essence, the narrative that Europeans introduced was that they were on a mission to transform the lives of the African people with an erroneous assumption to justify their character assassination.

It was established that Africans were pagans and, as a result, unrefined because they interpreted different God as a metaphysical phenomenon. Not giving room for alternative perspectives to spirituality thus led to the hostile condemnation of the African spiritual system so that they would have the moral right to continue with their nefarious activities. For a people who are dubbed as barbaric, primitive, savage, crude, and intellectually unrefined, the European expansionists placed themselves in the Big Brother position where they had the moral ground to "civilize" Africans. Even if the world was unsatisfied by the series of humanitarian atrocities committed by the West against Africans during the period, they were either facing similar troubling situations or were outright powerless to challenge them. After all, the West began Industrial Revolution, which gave them a superior technology that could be used for whatever reason they wanted. Africans struggled, they were browbeaten, challenged and confronted with consuming situations, but they were powerless. In all these times, their vilification and condemnation were going on unabated.

Whereas missionary works abetted slavery as that was the place where the moral justification for the action of the bestial Europeans was concocted, it nonetheless was incomparable to the next stage of moral suicide that they committed against the people. In the course of their ransacking of African civilization for slavery expedition, Europeans discovered that Africans were blessed with natural resources that they had never imagined. For instance, they discovered that the availability of gold in the Asante kingdom was so unprecedented in their experience, so much that they named the place Gold Coast. The irredeemable King Leopold of Belgium became enamored with the gold and other natural resources found in Congo and became so glued to it that he wrestled other Europeans to take control of the resources for years. The British government also discovered that the Nigerian space was fertile for all manners of agricultural products and would therefore become fixed on getting maximum gains from them. This therefore introduced colonialism to Africa as a way to consolidate the gains of the selfish imperialist. You should have noticed by now that the only way to continue with their domination was to persistently vilify, irrevocably slander and unapologetically dehumanize the African person so that they could have continued access to these resources.

While the above provides the economic justification for the vilification of Africans in the time past, it should be noticed too that there is another reason for the unceasing persecution of the African people by Europeans. This is what I call envy, and the following would establish my sentiment. Do you know, for instance, that the saying "Blacks don't crack" is credited to Americans, and it came from the knowledge that in spite of the limitless travails, hostilities, and persecution against Africans, they still did not bend or demonstrate any sign of defeat? In the American society where slaves were held, a series of slaves took opportunities to set themselves free and, in some cases, masterminded the escape of the entrapped others. People confronted all manners of hardship and frustration just so that they would continue to exist and defy all forms of European totalitarian approaches to them. They did not bend, and they had a biological structure that stood strong in spite of consuming challenges. The slave keeper would therefore wonder as to what was their source of inspiration and motivation. Eventually, they were incorporated as members of American society after the independence of the country but will later face a perpetual challenge of profiling, racism, and institutional warfare aimed at breaking them for whatever reason. The Blacks continued because they were naturally unbreakable.

Meanwhile, there is something about human psychology that the West discovered and used more than many other people. The West is aware that if you continue to say something about someone, even if it does not have a historical or scientific foundation, at a point in time, it would become the basis for which the ones affected by the narratives would begin to see themselves that way. This explains why someone would ask in the twenty-first century if something is inherently wrong with the African people. If the world is unsure of the rationality of the African people, the least that the people could do themselves would be to share such a mindset against themselves. In all honesty, they would have become good accessories to their own destruction when they began to think this way. At the same time, the African people are practically helpless, especially in coming to this conclusion. On a number of times, institutions that their forebears struggled to build were used against them, and they were powerless in stamping their voices. They are repressed and have continued to be the primary target of all manners of immoral or institutional decadence. That is the reason why they feel unsafe in most places where they are. Their detachment has made them suffer psychological consequences that they have to face even in contemporary times. In this way, the vilification of the African human is a necessity to keep the old order to continue.

Meanwhile, the in-house Africans are undergoing similar, if not worse humanitarian challenges. Given the understanding that colonialism was stopped not because the West was tired of forcefully taking the resources of the African people but because there was a global pressure that brought about the moral policing of activities of colonial engagement. The unpreparedness of the European government therefore compelled them to leave systems that would not function effectively for the people behind. Even when their countries were given independence, it appears that they were eternally tied to the apron strings of their ex-colonial imperialists, who exploited that opportunity on the economic and also political front. It led to the continuation of differences, boundary making, and delineation of cultures, among others which became commonplace in post-independence Africa and a recipe for unprecedented disasters. The Anglophone Africans would not find the need to conduct business with the francophone Africans, and vice versa, for a protracted period.

This would therefore open the door for manipulation and configuration of the people toward the wishes and aspirations of their controllers—the West.

If these people therefore considered internal contradictions in Africa as the means to continue in the exploitation of their resources, they would mastermind it or become accessories under different guises. You would remember that America imposed itself on the conduct of internal political affairs of Libya, which led to the untimely death of Mohammed Qaddafi, its President. Their occupation was argued as a demonstration of concerns about how a country decides to rule itself. Meanwhile, the same West would not decide to construct infrastructures for African countries that are suffering from resources deficit. They would not intervene to resolve issues from warring factions caused in the first place by the colonially imposed structures which they brought. The most apparent interpretation that this can get is that the continued persecution of the continent is a very lucrative business for the powerful or strong countries of the world. An unsettled Africa would always invite the attention of the West, which comes with its attendant consequences. They would want to continue in this way because there is a bundle of economic and financial advantages that they derive from the war-ridden continent.

Whereas it would appear that the blame for the misdirection of Africa should be exclusively shifted to the European or the West, when one understands the roles played by some Africans, one would come to the realization that they are ruthless accomplices to the challenges that they are facing. For all intent and purposes, all the military actions undertaken by the African military powers were taken by Africans themselves. While it is not impossible that they were motivated or sponsored by an unknown external body, their willingness to turn their countries into a theatre of blood so that they would have power underscored the reason for dehumanization. This means that they are ready to dehumanize the people themselves, and any external participant who has exploited that opportunity did so because the opportunity presented itself. The political class is not excluded from the eternal persecution of their people. In no better way would you talk about persecution than having leaders of a country take the money that belongs to the public and stash it somewhere in European banks and also in American businesses. All of these have continued to contribute to the ceaseless persecution, slander, and vilification of Africans in contemporary times.

The gradual declination of African moral culture that negated the habit of begging entirely was inspired vigorously by the deliberate administrative incapacity to diversify and develop the people's economy. Despite the awareness and understanding that Africa is one of the most gifted continents in the world, African leaders have showcased their mental inability to develop these things and make the best financial profits from the engagement. When untapped, natural resources become burdens to the people and could potentially impede them in the long run. When resources are left untapped and the available ones are mismanaged, it creates an enabling environment for crime. Where there are crimes, it breeds chaos and strives that would always make it unsafe for any form of economic engagement that can attract financial stability and prosperity or give the people their deserved advancement. The understanding that the culture of begging has become the order of the day is an omen for possible criminal activities in the future as the people would have the freedom to perpetuate problems and threaten the collective peace of the people. This means that the first level of people's collective moral collapse is then you see groups and traditions that are otherwise against the culture of begging now taking pride in it without feeling remorse.

The government is aware, but they are perpetually interested in an uninformed majority as that would help them solidly place themselves for opportunities where the children of the powerless would not have access to equal opportunities. They would have been disadvantaged by the conditions of their environment, which exposed them to innumerable risks and threatening situations. Begging does not come from people's admiration of that culture but from the feeling of defeat felt by individuals who have lost hope of possible redemption. However, as much as it has become a culture that people find attractive and lucrative, they begin to detest the idea of engaging in works that can bring them the financial fortress needed to plant themselves strong in their environment. Non-disabled individuals who are now pushed to the idea of begging are potential explosives that would destroy the future of Africans if appropriate measures are not immediately implemented. Underneath that practice is a self-defeating mentality that the culprits would assimilate. They would begin to see an increasing lack of capacity in themselves, which alone can motivate them to do unimaginable things. This wave of begging has signaled a new social challenge across the continent. From gold to uranium, crude oil to others, the deposit of natural resources in the continent indicates that the Africans are sitting on an eternal means of economic power. Apart from this, they are also blessed with limitless opportunities regarding their agricultural capabilities. They have arable land in moderate proportions and can generate humongous fortunes. Apart from this, they have engaging manpower with which they can also improve their economic conditions, but somehow, the political class has refused to put things that would facilitate the acceleration of projects that would transform these things into concrete results. Without investment into things, there would be a problem in maximizing the underlying opportunities. This is generally the case for many African countries with only a few exemptions. As long as the political class continues to get material benefits from the office, it does not matter if the ordinary is faced with varying challenges. The irony is that even when resources are waiting to be activated, exploited, and in that case, developed for the common good, even African leaders run to smaller countries to seek some financial rescue or the other. They have continued to run from one European country to another seeking financial assistance.

As if all the administrative atrocities that African leaders commit are not enough, they are all united in corruption. Although different academic research works have exposed the complicity of nearly all the politicians of the world in corrupt practices, however, the character of the African political class is different. Apart from mopping people's financial resources, African politicians are also involved in abuses of their offices. Meanwhile, their offices are abused, affecting all the institutions available. It is the result of office misuse that, for example, leads to the bloating of figures during project execution. Politicians connive with private organizations to sabotage progress by their actions of demanding gratification, kickbacks, and some unsubstantiated fees before they either award the projects or sign important documents. When they double-cross the process this way, the needed project would not be handled with a good sense of professionalism, in which case the innocent masses would bear the brunt. Instead of genuinely undertaking projects where the youths would participate in learning and getting necessary economic benefits, African politicians would rather devote the funds to frivolities that would have no particular purpose for the people. This is one of the enduring legacies of African politicians in the current time.

Projects where younger ones would demonstrate their intellectual capacity, would be awarded to their cronies, and instead of the masses being effectively carried along, they would be used for other things that promise them no purposeful returns. The money needed to develop the agricultural sector, where an average individual would potentially offer their mental and physical capabilities in exchange for financial benefits, would be denied such opportunities only to use them for their provincial intentions. As an alternative to survive, the innocent youths take severe measures to get access to money, including predominantly morally reprehensible engagements. The more corrupt the political class is, the more difficult it becomes for, the younger ones to survive economically. In essence, they are mostly drawn into activities that hold the community to ransom, increasing their worries and multiplying their despair. Those who do not have the courage to continue in that trajectory are pushed into begging, which adds to the statistics of Africans who desperately need immediate support. All these are what give the Western community the motivation to vilify the African people. I believe that the inadequate lack of economic power contributes to racism worldwide.

Sanya Osha: What are your views on reparations for Africans and peoples of African descent and how realizable is the idea as a global project?

Toyin Falola: Answer

Reparation restores people's confidence and rebuilds their emotions, but as much as it has very positive sides, there are negative aspects of reparation that make it an unworthy engagement. I have mixed views about reparation for African people, especially with regard to how it brings positive things to the people and their development trajectory. Africans were robbed of many things, including and especially their intellectual property, that would be very valuable in situating them in a good position for competition and inspiration. As I have already implied above, the European were miffed not only about the natural resources that they found in Africa during their time of expansionist agenda but also with the amazing level of human resources that are domiciled in the continent. The understanding that a people can be forward-looking and have deep thoughts enthused the West to the point of carting to their place the innumerable creative works that were done by the

Africans. Of course, the intention might not have been to starch these possessions into museums to gather money for themselves in the future. Apparently, it could be for their own artistic appreciation and, in some cases, the knowledge that they can draw from the said objects. One of the positive sides of reparation is that people whose indigenous artifacts and artistic works were stolen and returned would maintain a good level of intellectual redefinition. Subsequent to the ceaseless persecution of African people that they were devoid of any intellectual value, the people have suffered limitless consequences of identity devaluation and character assassination, the combination of which have come with extreme psychological consequences for them. They have continued to face internal contradictions and ravaging challenges over the understanding that the image associated with them is a demeaning one, which makes them lose value and names in the presence of others the world over. This is particularly understandable, for example, if you are accused of being an empty mind that is incapable of forward-thinking, and you protest that you have a backlog of things that have been achieved in your lineage, the most important way of convincing the people would be to provide evidence for all the things which you said you have achieved in the time past. While people can indulge you and listen to your side of the story, convincing them then depends on the evidence you supply to support your argument. But when this is not forthcoming, you lose your respect. Africans have begun the protest against the negative narratives that have been peddled against them for a long time but have continued to achieve less success because they lack concrete evidence to back their claims up. Meanwhile, it is difficult to rely on the West to redeem the image of a people which they consciously and constantly invested in its mudslinging. Knowing this, Africans began to protest in every way they could important, which among other things, led to the coal for the reparation for them in all manners. Their agitation is strengthened by the awareness that any civilization that is involved in the decapitation of others should make some form of restitution to them so that victims would have some sense of relief. While some groups of individuals or races that suffered severe deprecation from the West have been compensated in one way or the other while Africans have not been given the necessary treatment they deserved. Some civilizations were given money, while the mode of reparations for others was different. However, Africans have continued to be neglected for whatever reason. All these have extended their emotional turbulence under the impression that they were a long target of Western deracination for political and economic reasons. They have continued to protest, but it seems that the West is unperturbed. A reparation to them would be a relief.

Apart from the restoration of their confidence, reparations for the valuables stolen or forcefully taken from Africa would come with economic advantages. It is a generally known fact that the people with whom these values and artifacts derive maximum financial gains from them as tourists come to visit them while researchers also make use of them for academic purposes. In these cases, they are getting maximum financial benefits from them. Meanwhile, this has constituted a great source of revenue generation in their countries. In Europe, for example, these values have been used to get large financial benefits from the people. Quite a number of people troop in there every time to view these things and derive some form of pleasure from them. In all the time when such has been the case, they have left Africans, who are the original copyright owners of these artifacts to derive no particular advantage from them. This is absolutely a demonstration of supremacist behavior that allows the West to be unapologetic with their obvious imposing and diabolical tendencies. Whereas Africans continue to employ all the means necessary to ask for the reclamation of these for reasons that are sometimes unconnected to the understanding that they are spiritual and economical values in the continent itself.

There is a general consensus that tourist-induced artifacts would always come with expansive and required economic and social development. When there are creative works that can draw the attention of people to a place, there would be efforts for the quick transformation of the place in its infrastructure and other development. This means that once there are things that would draw tourists to come over to a particular place, they would also have the motivation to improve their sociopolitical conditions as that would determine the extent to which they would attract more individuals. In essence, there is a direct correlation between releasing their artifacts to them and instantly getting the necessary financial advantages. One would almost ask as to the reason for the refusal to grant these people the heritage which they concede belongs to them. But since they are also using that part of the reasons for getting increased economic values, one would therefore understand the reason for their refusal to get them back. From observation, reparations of these valuable objects would promote instant financial gains as activities that would be developed from them are almost limitless. Many people have always believed that with these African artifacts returned to them, they would garner many economic benefits. As such, my positive view about reparations is that it would attract many economic gains for the ones who have the original copyright rights to the possessions. However, as there are positive sides to reparations, there are also some negative sides to it that are to be evenly considered. One of the leading negative sides of reparations is that these objects, when returned, would most predictably lose their value in no time. I should state clearly that losing their value when returned to Africans is not informed by the incapacity of Africans to manage them. The problem comes from the lack of adequate infrastructural resources with which they can be preserved the way they are being preserved in the Western world. This problem comes from knowing that many African governments are entirely not concerned about the well-being of these things. In fact, the government is yet to take appropriate measures to improve the conditions of humans that are in serious need of administrative and political ideas that would increase their value. It would thus be an illusion to expect that such government would place high values on artifacts that would be kept in museums and other archival storage facilities. It would be noticed that the quest for reparations is mostly done by individuals and groups who believe that they are entitled to the intellectual property of their forebears. In spite of their agitations, however, these artifacts would not be released to these groups or individuals as it is more formal to handle them to governments of these countries.

Even when there are increased agitations that people want their artifacts returned back to them so that they would be in their possession, it is fundamental to consider the sociopolitical process of its return. The politicians who have divested in social welfare will not particularly be concerned if some artifacts are well kept in the museums or not. We would understand how disinterested many African governments are when we evaluate their diversification tendency in recent history. Many of them are dependent on a single source of economic engagement, and for this reason, they continue to undermine all other sources of economic sustenance and financial restoration. Their constant and continued derivation of financial needs from a source, for example, Nigeria's crude oil, has blinded their capacity to think in creative ways on how they can facilitate more funds through other means available. This is the case because the political class is self-sufficient, and they have refused to respond to the challenges of the masses, which would have been answered by concentrating on other areas of income generation. Without placing their focus on diverse ways of generating money, it would be difficult for them to preserve and maintain these artifacts on the occasion that they are returned as envisaged.

Aside from the possibility of its destruction, the reparations for Africans in terms of money would have a negative impact on them, especially again because of their political conditions. Accountability is one of the things that are not available in many African countries. Leaders are unaccountable and would always rub their administrative atrocities on innocent citizens. For government officials who are not accountable to their people in the management of the meager resources available to them, it will be counter-productive to expect such a government to have the interest of the people at heart when offered opportunities that the majority of the people do not even know existed. Nigeria has been given a humongous sum of money which they tag as the money laundered to Western countries by some of their past political leaders. In spite of this development, there has been a deficit of accountability to the people eventually. This means that these funds are, in most cases, mismanaged. Therefore, if the political class cannot maintain basic decency to manage available resources to assist or improve the conditions of their environment, how then would one expect that they would effectively manage a fund you call reparations? In whatever form the reparations are made, my views as laid in the above would have suggested to you that I hold an indifferent position given the circumstances and conditions that would be tied to them as highlighted. At the global level, there would be a reassurance that the yearnings of people are listened to, which would be an important signal to underpin their desire to correct many things which have been masterminded against them for a number of years. In the same vein, however, one would see that it comes with challenges of unimaginable proportion as reparations could potentially distract the governments in Africa. Although the money would be of positive addition if managed effectively, it does not remove the fact of emotional damage that the people had suffered. I mean, how do you pay back someone whom you have defiled their dignity, raped their honor, and broken their spirits?

Of course, there may be some positive sides to it when viewed from a different perspective, but I am of the opinion that the best way for repatriation would be that they should be allowed to take charge of their political and economic engagement without manipulating them or imposing on them on how they should run their affairs. That may potentially lead them to true freedom.

Sanya Osha: What aspects of your life and work are you most proud of?

Toyin Falola: Answer
You see, life is full of complexities that are sometimes difficult to navigate when there is no solid motivation and encouragement that would continue to energize one in the process. Although there is a universal definition of success, one thing that I have come to realize is that every individual has a definition of success that they carve for themselves, and as soon as they achieve these goals and objectives, they would be enough as evidence of success in their own right. With respect to myself, it is based on the awareness that I have achieved my set goals in the various aspects that I would thus consider myself as successful. In essence, I can say that the first aspect of my life that I am continuously proud of is my marriage and the successful children that I have.

As a child, one would not understand the dimensions and layers of complexity of life until one begins to get immersed in the activities and events of life. By this ignorance, one at that stage would have a definition of success that is sometimes removed from human reality. One of such realities is that, as Africans, at a point, one begins to understand that one's life belongs to not only oneself but a group of people whose lives are culturally and emotionally tied. These groups consist of one's wife, one's children, and members of the family that are added as one grows up.

No matter how a man achieves material success, without a happy family and successful children, one cannot boast of achieving anything worth his salt as an individual. In fact, there are many sayings in the Yorùbá world that corroborate this assertion. As a scholar and an academic, for that matter, to have a happy marriage is one of the most valuable things to one's life's trajectory. This is so because writers are thinkers and by the nature of their engagements, they do not naturally need to be disturbed by distractive things in whatever disguise. Writers have to think and conduct research and would be so disadvantaged on the occasion that their thinking is occasionally distracted by other inevitable commitments.

It requires a good soulmate who would understand you and be ready to complement you in whatever capacity they can. It is the sacrifices that are required from both parties that sometimes scare some people away from the institution of marriage. That I have a happy marriage is something I cherish in my life as that has helped strengthen my career in very many ways. Imagine I have an uncooperative wife, how would it have been easy to continue to shuttle between America and different African countries with the intention to advance them by adding values to them? I am successful because I have a happy marriage, and that success is reinforced by having successful children too.

Another very memorable thing in my life and career is having colleagues who are always ready to be of help to my engagements. I think it is not an understatement when I say, for instance, that I would not have achieved maximally if I had not been blessed with great colleagues. There is a saying that no foreman has the ability to do the work of four men. No matter how versatile I think I am and what I can do at a time, if I had been plagued by unprogressive colleagues in my world, I would not have been close to whatever I have achieved today. My gratefulness to them comes in handy for so many reasons. Through your colleagues, you would be aware of your capabilities and how limitless you are. They are always available to provide you with the hard truth which you need to advance yourself. They are your primary critic, and their opinions would not be coming from the angle of hate. They are concerned, like you, about how individuals would be of immense influence to the world and generally contribute to the events of their environment. Where I am, my colleagues have facilitated my growth by helping me in many ways that I had never imagined. They are helpful, important, and have an imposing outlook on my academic and career engagements. For this reason, it is actually an important addition to me and my intellectualism as the lack of their contribution and support would have come with consequences.

In another instance, I have been immeasurably successful in the area of impacting the educational policies of many countries. In fact, my writings and academic arguments have been made the basis for a review of some hitherto unprofitable and unproductive policies that have not yielded maximally for the people. In many African countries, the reevaluation of their academic curriculum has been triggered by various scholarly positions that I have championed. Although several scholars have done similar laudable things in the past and present moments, the fact that I am instrumental in the establishment of value and valuable ideas have added to my joy. In all modesty, my research works and findings have always been used for several purposes, both in the public and private sectors. Tertiary institutions have keyed into the ideas and arguments we have raised, and many economic groups have derived happiness in making use of my intellectual property. This gives a significant impression and has been a solid motivation for the activities that I am involved with in my life. The fact of impacting policies is not as joyous and satisfactory as when you realize that your ideas brought about success when and where they are adopted. In many places where my ideas have been incorporated as policies, the fact that they have achieved success brings reassurance.

To my career, I think working in a non-competitive mind framework has also brought about great success for me and my career. In my mental frame, I appreciate the growth that every other person is making, and the respect, whether mutual or not, does not bother me. In that case, I am not either overtly or covertly involved in any rat race where I want to outdo the other or be like them. The environment affords me the opportunity to be myself and achieve my fullest potential. I am not evaluated based on how far I can challenge the others with whom I am in the same career trajectory. Instead, it is based on what I can offer and, in a way, how I can be of immense value to the institution I work with specifically and the environment in which I work generally. With the understanding that I need to be myself, I have found the motivation to compete with myself, which gives me the opportunity to increase myself in value and content. In as much as I am aware that where I get to in life depends on how well I am ready to squeeze myself and be uncomfortable with the comfort zone where I am, I renew my energy to continue to become the best version of myself. I have therefore undertaken tasks that would definitely bring me the needed light to reconfigure myself in different ways. More than you would have imagined, I have been able to increase my values because of this system.

In spite of the available responsibilities ahead of me, I have count as evidence of success the fact that I navigate easily between my career and social engagement. My social life is not boring as you would have in some academics. This has helped strengthen my academic awareness more. It is through my social involvement, for example, that I came to discover some interesting things about my career. Being a historian, sometimes what you need to conduct research engagement is a spark that would, in some cases, come from the network you have. In essence, being confined exclusively to academic engagements and therefore denying oneself the values and ideals involved in being socially informed would be a negative addition to one's career generally, and that would be greatly devastating for a historian. In spite of working in North America, I have come to Africa to witness a number of their cultural and social events, and that has deepened my understanding of some very important things. Beyond that, the conferment of chieftaincy titles to me is proof that social life has certainly come with its numerous advantages. What I am saying is that being very social and functioning effectively as an academic at the same time has been an added advantage and what I celebrate in my career trajectory.

Within the period of my academic career and engagements, I have traveled far and wide on the continent of Africa to participate in the transformational process of the countries. I have given public lectures and have mediated on political issues through my intellectual exchanges. That has increased my own credibility among my people, and I must be frank with you that it gives me joy. I cannot understate the importance of this to my existence. People see my work and also feel my presence has been a blessing to my family generally. Because of these involvements, several academic conferences have been organized in my honor and in my name on many occasions. People are encouraged by the mere awareness that an African like them is pushing the frontiers of knowledge in the global community. I have attended occasions in countries where I would have ordinarily not imagined, and that was because the influence of my works is felt in many places. I have continued to be a reference point for people who want their wards to do well and a model for academics who desire to accomplish better in their life aspirations. This has become a valid reason for the continuation of my efforts as I have resolved to give my best in whatever capacity I can make. I am particularly proud that people have accepted their cultural identity because I play a role.

Lastly, the understanding that I am involved in the lives of many younger members of the coming generation of Africans gives me unexplainable joy. Training the next generation of scholars and showing them how they should navigate their educational career gives profound happiness as one is drawn close to them to understand what they are capable of from a close range. I get to understand their fears. I also get to know their capabilities and use my experience and skills to direct them and influence their behavior in life. All of these have given me joy of inestimable value, and I am proud that I have taken their route in life.

INDEX

Aaro culture 130
abiku 7
accountability 55, 59, 175
Achebe, C. 6, 143
activism 102, 104
   LGBTIQI+, 24
   social 15, 24
Ade Ajayi, J. F. 119
Adichie, C. N. 84
Africa
   colonial economy in 64
   cultural history 81
   cultural traditions 104
   dignity 82
   epistemology of 24, 117
   feminisms 20
   identity 89, 91, 97, 144
   indigenous ontological ideas 141
   intellectual culture 154–62
   knowledge institution 74
   religion 141
   reparations for 171–6
   renaissance 15, 88
   sociopolitical and sociocultural pace 96
   spirituality 154
   values 96, 108, 141, 144, 145
   vilification 162–71
   weltanschuung 23
African memoirs and cultural representations (Falola) 13
African National Congress (ANC) 16, 17
African Spirituality, Politics, and Knowledge Systems: Sacred Words and Holy Realms (Falola) 12
African Union (AU) 15, 91
Afrocentric theory 34, 91

Afrofuturism 34
Afropolitanism, concept of 12
Agbekoya 61–70
Aje 161
Akosejaiye 122, 123
ala 31, 38
alienation 24, 26
almajiri culture 124
Anglophones 17, 33, 167
Anikulapo-Kuti, F. 156
anthropology 3, 11, 24, 106, 139, 146, 157, 159
anti-Semitism 20
Arabophone 33
are 25
art theory 3
Awe, B. 119
Awolowo, O. 65
awure 7
Àyànmó 121, 151

babalawo 7, 8
Bible 146
black cultures
   Caribbean 3
   South America 3
blackness
   concept of 11
   ideologies of 21

Cesaire, A. 12
civilization 61, 71, 82, 88, 89, 125, 127, 129, 143, 150, 160, 172, 173
   African 156, 164
   Western 95, 107
   Yorùbá 62, 123
   in Yorùbáland 57

colonialism 3, 19, 20, 33, 98, 140, 156, 165, 166
communalism 3, 23, 26, 32, 38
Communism 88
communitarianism 26
compartmentalization 24
competence 133, 134
confidence 67, 84, 94, 125, 133, 136, 137, 148, 171, 173
conscientiousness 59, 133–5
consciousness 23, 149, 151, 152, 155
cosmology 10, 148–54
cosmopolitanism 10, 19, 22, 24, 38
Counting the Tiger's Teeth (Falola) 61, 62
COVID-19 pandemic 15
Critique of Black Reason (Mbembe) 11
crude oil 142, 164, 169
cultural identity 64, 123, 125, 147, 181
cultural traditions 71, 80, 86, 104, 106, 123, 128, 147
cultures 4, 9, 13, 33, 56, 78, 155, 157, 167
  black 3

decolonization 3, 95, 143, 148
Decolonizing African Knowledge (Falola) 13
Deleuze, G. 11
devotion 55, 60
digital globalization 11
dignity 58, 61, 63, 64, 77, 82, 98, 106, 128, 131, 176
Dike, K. O. 119
diligence 55, 59, 137
Discourse on Colonialism (Cesaire) 12

Economic Community of West African States (ECOWAS) 33
economics 61, 63, 85, 87, 89, 92, 96, 98, 126, 128–30, 140, 141, 155, 165, 167, 168, 170, 173, 175, 176, 179
  growth 90, 118, 146
  power 169, 171
  power of colonial system 64
  profits 67
  security 63
  values 68, 78, 174
  of West African region 33
education 70–75, 79, 80, 82, 85, 89, 95, 97, 103, 108, 109, 115, 147
  in South Africa 15

eesun 30
egungun (masquerade) 10
Eledumare 152
emere 7
emotional intelligence 133, 137, 138
encouragement 146, 177
English culture 79
episteme 10
epistemology 10, 21, 28, 71, 82, 117, 147, 154, 155
  chauvinism 33
  ethics 10
  of holism 23
ethnology 3
Eurocentrism 116, 144, 145
Europe 26, 63
  black cultures in 3
  colonialism 13
  cultural 10

fairness 55, 60, 125, 157
Falola, T. 3, 100, 127, 133, 138, 149, 154, 162, 171, 177
  Interviews 4, 15, 31, 33, 34, 37
Fanon, F. 38
fertility 62, 79
fragmentation 24
Francophones 17, 33, 142, 167
Fulani aggression (1840) 63

G8, 15
Galileo 99
gender studies 3
globalization 9, 11, 73, 141
  studies 3
gods 30
gold 165, 169
Gontran-Damas, L. 12

health care 24
Hermes 6
hieroglyphics 30
History of the Yoruba (Johnson) 9
HIV/Aids 15, 16
holism, epistemology of 23, 28
honesty 55, 60, 127, 128, 166
humanism 4
humanities 3, 24, 70
humility 55, 60

hungry 95
Hussein, S. 99
hyper-digitalization 24, 34

Ibadan 7, 24, 25, 31, 32, 55, 57, 63, 111
   communalism 32
   history of 57
Ifa 10
Independent National Electoral
   Commission (INEC) 33
Industrial Revolution 164
"In remembrance of the slave" (Osha) 5
inspiration 73, 81, 154, 157, 160, 165, 171
integrity 58, 120, 133, 135, 138
intellectualism 82, 103, 105, 113, 178
interculturality 19–28, 38
interdisciplinary
   in nature 79–88
   in scope 79–88
international relations 24
iron 170
Iyemoja 161

Jesus 101
Johnson, S. 9, 144–8
Joyce, J. 38

Kant, I. 105
knowledge 4, 24, 25, 26, 31, 38, 60, 61,
   67–71, 73, 74, 77, 80–82, 84, 85,
   92, 98, 101, 102, 104, 105, 108, 113,
   114, 117, 120, 122, 124, 133, 145,
   147, 151, 155, 157–60, 165, 172, 181
   academic attention 146
   of biology 152
   of creative writing 87
   social interaction 134
   of sociology 86

Leku 120–7
LGBTIQI+ activism 24
LGBTQI+ community 26
life and career 177–81
literary criticism 3
logos 38
loyalty 55, 91, 142, 153
Lusophone 33

Mandela, N. 16, 37
Marx, K. 38

Mbeki, T. 15–18
Mbembe, A. 11
Mesiogo 7
missionary 6, 163, 164
modernity 7, 11, 32, 35, 127–33, 144–8
mogbas 30
Mohammed 101
moral ideology 56, 58
motivation 74, 82, 84, 127, 165, 171, 174,
   177, 179
A Mouth Sweeter than Salt (Falola) 32, 120–7
multidisciplinary education 81

nationalist bigotry 33
natural resources 66, 93, 165, 168,
   169, 171
Negritude movement 90
neocolonialism 3, 13, 15, 98, 156, 157
Nigeria 32, 33, 56, 57, 66, 70, 100, 101,
   104, 106, 112, 117, 142, 175, 176
   INEC 34
   military regimes in 77
   Obafemi Awolowo University (OAU) 71
   politics 79
   post-independence 126
   schools 76
Nkrumah, K. 17, 18
North America 104, 106, 108, 109, 180
Nyerere, J. 17

Obafemi Awolowo University (OAU) 142
   centrality of 71
   faculty power 73
   "For Learning and Culture", 71
   humanities 70
   ideological values 72
   social sciences 70
   teachers and colleagues attitude to
      education 75–76
   theoretical ideas and knowledge 71
   undergraduate students in 74–75
Obatala 29
odundun 30
Odunjo, J. F. 144–8
ogede 13
Ogun 29, 31, 160
ogun owo 7
ojubo 30
Olokun 29

Oloruntoba, S. 12
Omoluabi 58, 59
ona-mogba 30
ontology 71, 120, 141, 149, 154, 164
Oogun (charms/juju) 67
The Organisation of African Unit 91
ori 10, 151, 152
orisa 10, 29–35, 160
orisa wiwe 30
Osayin 161
Osha, S. 55, 61, 70, 79, 88, 93, 99, 104, 110, 115, 120, 127, 148, 154, 162, 177
osii-mogba 30
Osoosi 29
Osun 29, 161
otuun-mogba 30
Oya 161

Pan-Africanism 15, 34, 88–93
  practice 3
  theory 3
The Paris Review 6
philosophy 3, 10, 11, 24, 26, 32, 55, 57, 75, 79, 86, 94, 125, 129, 132, 133, 136, 138, 144, 160, 162
  individualism 159
  social 150, 162
pluralism 24
poetry 3
political science 3, 24
political security 63
postcolonial governance 20
post-Fordist capitalism 11
power 8, 12, 25, 58, 64–69, 73, 76, 91, 98, 104, 107, 124, 150, 156, 161, 163
  African military 168
  of collectivism 64
  cosmological 122
  economic 64, 130, 169, 171
  financial 130, 142
  political 156
  spirituality 13
  of technology 97
primitivism 24

Qaddafi, M. 167

racism 20, 33, 166, 171
radicalism 76

Ransom Kuti, O. 156
reciprocity 3, 31, 38
religion 10, 11, 29, 30, 94, 101, 120, 125, 140
  intolerance 33
respect 55, 58, 59, 61, 64, 66, 68, 72, 104, 126, 130, 132, 133, 136–8, 151, 172, 177, 179
#RhodesMustFall movement 14

Sango 29–31, 161
Sankofa, concept of 9
schizophrenia 13
scholarship 3, 38, 84, 85, 92, 104, 108, 115–20, 154
  interculturality 19–28
  transdisciplinarity 19–28
Senghor, L. S. 12, 17, 165
sexuality studies 24
slave/slavery 3, 90, 145, 161–5
  in Africa 13
  transatlantic slave trade 10, 32
  trans-Saharan slave trade 10
social activism 15, 24
social interactions 56, 95, 134
social sciences 3, 70
social security 63
socialism 78
sociocultural movement 92
sociology 3, 10, 24, 85, 87, 126, 131, 154
socio-political process 175
Socrates 94
Soyinka, W. 143, 150
spirituality 24, 121, 140, 148–54
  orisa 29, 30
  Yoruba people 24

tax policy 63, 66, 69
tete 30
TFI series 33, 34
Thoth (Tehuti) 30
"Three recent books that explain the work of Nigeria's famous decolonial scholar" (Osha) 6
"Toyin Falola at seventy: A pan-Africanist luminary for the digital age" (Osha) 5
Toyin Falola Conference (TOFAC) 108
"Toyin Falola's enchanted universe" (Osha) 6
transatlantic slave trade 10, 19, 29, 32

transdisciplinarity 5, 38
  scholarship of 19–28
transformational process 9, 10, 20, 57, 61, 62, 64, 135, 147, 161, 174, 180
trans-humanism 34
transnationality 19, 21, 22
transnationalization 19, 21, 22
trans-Saharan slave trade 10
truthfulness 55, 59

Ubuntu, philosophy of 4, 161, 162
United States 19
  black cultures in 3
University of Ife. *See* Obafemi Awolowo University (OAU)
uranium 169

violence 10, 16, 17, 62, 64
volte faces 38

Western civilization 129
Western education 66, 70, 72, 79, 82, 141, 145, 160. *See also* education
Western medical system 159
Wiredu, K. 25

xenophobia 15, 33

Yemoja 29
Yoruba 100, 102
  chieftaincy titles 110–15
  cosmology 148–54
  culture 9, 11, 29, 32, 33, 58, 61–70, 127–33
  epistemological and cosmological framework 10
  Fulani aggression 63
  history of 9, 11, 61
  identity 11
  language 32, 58, 146
  metaphysics 82, 83
  moral ideology 58
  moral lifestyle of 56
  origins 9
  regional power 66
  sociocultural settlemen 57
  spirituality 13, 148–54
  values 55
Yorùbáland
  chieftaincy titles in 115
  civilization in 57

zeitgeist 34

www.ingramcontent.com/pod-product-compliance
Lightning Source LLC
Jackson TN
JSHW022149240525
84171JS00001B/3